Making
Connections
with Blogging

Authentic Learning for
Today's Classrooms

Lisa Parisi
Brian Crosby

LB1044.87.P37 2012
Parisi, Lisa.
Making connections with
blogging : authentic
learning for today's
classrooms
Eugene, Or. : International

International Society for Technology in Education
EUGENE, OREGON • WASHINGTON, DC

Making **Connections** with **Blogging**
Authentic Learning for Today's Classrooms

Lisa Parisi and Brian Crosby

Director of Book Publishing: *Courtney Burkholder*
Acquisitions Editor: *Jeff V. Bolkan*
Production Editors: *Tina Wells, Lynda Gansel*
Production Coordinator: *Emily Reed*
Graphic Designer: *Signe Landin*
Copy Editor: *Davis N. Smith*
Proofreader: *Kathy Hamman*
Indexer: *Ken Hassman*
Illustrations, Cover Design, Book Design, and Production: *Sandy Kupsch*

Library of Congress Cataloging-in-Publication Data
Parisi, Lisa.
  Making connections with blogging : authentic learning for today's classrooms / Lisa Parisi and Brian Crosby. — 1st ed.
    p. cm.
  Includes index.
  ISBN 978-1-56484-312-8 (pbk.)
  1. Internet in education. 2. Blogs. I. Crosby, Brian (Brian Paul) II. Title.
  LB1044.87.P37 2012
  371.33'44678—dc23

                                                    2011051287

First Edition
ISBN: 978-1-56484-312-8
Printed in the United States of America

ISTE® is a registered trademark of the International Society for Technology in Education.

About ISTE

The International Society for Technology in Education (ISTE) is the trusted source for professional development, knowledge generation, advocacy, and leadership for innovation. ISTE is the premier membership association for educators and education leaders engaged in improving teaching and learning by advancing the effective use of technology in PK–12 and teacher education.

Home to ISTE's annual conference and exposition, the ISTE leadership conference, and the widely adopted NETS, ISTE represents more than 100,000 professionals worldwide. We support our members with information, networking opportunities, and guidance as they face the challenge of transforming education. To find out more about these and other ISTE initiatives, visit our website at www.iste.org.

As part of our mission, ISTE Book Publishing works with experienced educators to develop and produce practical resources for classroom teachers, teacher educators, and technology leaders. Every manuscript we select for publication is carefully peer reviewed and professionally edited. We value your feedback on this book and other ISTE products. Email us at books@iste.org.

International Society for Technology in Education
Washington, DC, Office:
    1710 Rhode Island Ave. NW, Suite 900, Washington, DC 20036-3132
Eugene, Oregon, Office:
    180 West 8th Ave., Suite 300, Eugene, OR 97401-2916
Order Desk: 1.800.336.5191
Order Fax: 1.541.302.3778
Customer Service: orders@iste.org
Book Publishing: books@iste.org
Book Sales and Marketing: booksmarketing@iste.org
Web: www.iste.org

About the Authors

 **Lisa Parisi** is a highly qualified classroom teacher, dual certified in general and special education. Working in the Herricks Union Free School District on Long Island, New York, she has been helping students be successful for more than 25 years. She began blogging with her students in 2007 and has been going strong with technology ever since. Lisa's classroom is run using the Universal Design for Learning (UDL) approach. She believes that all students can be successful, given the right tools and time. She uses technology to help her students reach their highest potential.

Lisa spends her free time running a Global Awareness Club for students, helping them to see the world in different ways. She also presents at conferences on UDL and project-based learning. And she enjoys teaching classes in her district to help other teachers learn to use technology in their classrooms.

Lisa and her students have won many awards, including the SIGTEL Online Learning award for global projects. Her articles have been published in *Scholastic* magazine, *Tech4Learning*, and various online sites. She is an EdTechTalk webcaster and the co-host of a weekly education webcast called Conversations. She blogs for The Secret Life of Scientists and Teaching Tolerance, as well as in her own blog, Lisa's Lingo. She is also a STAR Discovery Educator, a SMART Exemplary Educator, a Glogster ambassador, a Voki ambassador, and a Fablevision ambassador. All of these extras help her keep up with technology in the classroom.

 **Brian Crosby**, a certified upper elementary teacher for 30 years, guides the learning in a classroom in Sparks, Nevada. Coming from a background in outdoor education and educational technology, Brian fuses his at-risk students' use of technology with field trips, art, hands-on activities, and a problem-based approach to build their schema of the world, while connecting them to it.

Brian's students are acclaimed for the community service projects they accomplish and he espouses. He believes children are valuable resources, and when they are seen learning while doing important work, society will be more willing to invest in them.

Brian is a community leader and writer for Powerful Learning Practice, an educator professional development company. He also blogs occasionally for the *The Huffington Post* as well as writes his own blog, Learning Is Messy. Brian and his students have won many awards, including an Apple iLife Award for their video "Don't Laugh at Me."

Brian also has created a wiki website to increase the learning at a local animal park, developed an advertising campaign for a nonprofit that recycles bicycles, and produced award-winning public service announcements about diversity and bullying.

Acknowledgments

There have been many quality people who have supported and assisted us throughout our journey into blogging and writing. Sue Waters, of Edublogs, was invaluable, teaching us about the many benefits of Edublogs and sharing examples of many educational blogs. Kim Cofino and Scott McLeod both contributed to many of the blog lists you can find in this book. David Warlick, of Class Blogmeister, is not only the best and most responsive webmaster of all time, but was incredibly supportive as we worked through the book. And thanks to our online personal learning network (PLN) for your patience with our queries and your quick responses to our link requests. We couldn't have done it without you!

Dedications

To Frank and Alixandra Parisi for all their patience and support throughout this project and always. —LP

To Nancy, Alana, and Kailyn Crosby (and, of course, Abby, our dog), who gave me the time, support, and encouragement to take on and follow through on my first book. —BC

Contents

Contents

Introduction

What we want is to see the child in pursuit of knowledge, and not knowledge in pursuit of the child.

—George Bernard Shaw

Blogging Hooks Students

"Welcome to blogging!" These words, spoken by the teacher in September, were met with excitement, trepidation, and anticipation among a class of fifth grade students.

One student, Monica, put her head on her desk and cried. Monica struggles with writing. She has been a classified special education child with an individualized education program (IEP) since first grade, focusing each year on the physical aspect of handwriting and the more difficult skill of putting words together to make cohesive paragraphs. Now in fifth grade, Monica has learned one thing about writing: she hates it. Most of the time, while the rest of the class is writing, Monica is using typical avoidance techniques—she heads to the bathroom, sharpens her pencil over and over, or simply cries. This has worked for her in the past, and she's ready to try it again this year. Blogging, she knows, is just another form of writing, and she is not interested at all.

But in this classroom, she has no choice. So with the teacher's assistance and much complaining, Monica pounds out a short paragraph about her goals for the year. Then her teacher shows her how to copy her paragraph and paste it into her blog. Done. Except the teacher is not finished; she sends out a message to other teachers who blog and asks them to comment on this student's first blog post.

The next day, Monica comes into class and reluctantly pulls up her blog. She sees that there are now several comments. Together, the class looks at the comments. One is from New Zealand! Where is New Zealand? Monica grabs an atlas, finds New Zealand, and clicks on the comment's link back to the commenter to learn more about her.

Monica is hooked.

In the same classroom, we have Steve. Steve is at the top of the class. He attends accelerated classes twice a week for enrichment. Steve is used to doing well in school. But the way Steve does well in school is by doing exactly what the teacher asks of him—no more and no less. So when the first blog assignment was given, Steve dutifully completed a perfect essay about his goals for the year. He had an introduction, a clear and focused body paragraph, and a perfect conclusion. His post was not terribly creative or interesting, but he did what was asked.

Next to Steve sits Mario. Mario is not a classified child, nor is he a gifted student. He is an average fifth grader who loves some assignments and hates others. But Mario always tries his best, no matter what the activity, and he is excited about this new blogging idea. He cheerfully writes his goals for the year, adding his own funny comments into the essay. He posts the essay and waits.

Both Steve and Mario, after seeing Monica's comments, decide to check their own blogs. Mario has quite a few comments. Many other children thought he was funny and told him how much they enjoyed his blog. Mario immediately sets out to write another post, even though it has not been assigned. He is anxious to get more comments. He also navigates to the blogs of his commenters. One child, he discovers, is a girl from Israel. She writes a blog about her favorite video games, and Mario sees that she enjoys the same games as he does. Mario comments on this child's post about a particular game, and thus begins a great year with his new blogging buddy.

Steve, on the other hand, does not find any comments. He notices that there are quite a few students in the class who received comments. In fact, he is watching Mario, who seems to have gotten the most. Steve is intrigued. He is also extremely competitive. He decides to read Mario's blog. He notes that Mario didn't have a conclusion to his post and spelled a few words wrong and that the post is funny. Laugh-out-loud funny. Steve decides to change his post a bit, adding more of himself into the blog entry. He resubmits it and waits for comments.

All three students are now caught up in blogging. And for them, writing will never be the same.

~~~

What Is Blogging?

According to the *American Heritage Dictionary* (4th ed., 2006), a *blog* (formerly *web-log*) is "A website containing the writer's or group of writers' own experiences, observations, opinions, etc., and often having images and links to other websites." Simple. But for educational purposes, blogging is so much more than simply a site of chronologically posted writings. It is a place for students to practice their writing and communication skills. It is a place where syntheses of ideas can take place. It is a tool used to encourage demonstration of ideas and learning. It is where students begin to build a global personal learning network (PLN). How can blogging be all that and so much more?

If you are new to the concept of blogging, the first thing to do is to go out and read some blogs! There are blogs on every conceivable topic. Are you a runner? Read some running blogs. Do you like to make pottery? Read pottery blogs. Do you enjoy politics? There are blogs covering every conceivable viewpoint. Next, read some blogs written by educators. Check out some classroom blogs written by students. All of these may be easily found via simple Internet searches. After you've read several blogs over a week or two, you will be well versed on what it is to blog. Maybe you'll even be inspired to post a comment or two!

You'll see that blogging is simply a form of publishing short posts, usually around a particular topic. Posts are made up of text, links to other content, and embedded content such as pictures and videos. The best blog authors post regularly, and good blog authors usually have loyal readers who often comment about the posts. Blog authors often read and comment on other blogs on similar topics, creating a blogging community.

Who Should Blog?

As you may have surmised from the opening vignette, blogging is unparalleled as a tool to keep motivating students to write. In fact, in our many years of teaching, it is the best motivator we have ever experienced. But is blogging for you? Is blogging something your students should be doing? Who benefits from blogging?

Should you be blogging if you teach mainly students from high socioeconomic backgrounds? Should students from high poverty backgrounds be blogging? What about special education or special needs students? How about gifted and talented students? What role does age play in blogging? Should younger students blog? Older ones?

The answer is that blogging is for everyone!

How do you manage blogging if you have only a few computers in your classroom? What if your students have access to computers at home but not much at school? Or maybe your students don't have access to the Internet at home, but they all do at school. Should they still be blogging? Maybe you only teach a single subject, such as math or science or social studies or PE. Should your students be blogging? Yes! We will show you how blogging can work in all these situations.

Naturally, students working on writing skills should blog. If your students need to practice usage or punctuation or word choice skills, then they should blog. And reading fits well. So if your students are working on reading comprehension and writing about what they've read, then they should be blogging. But if you also believe it is important that your students learn to be critical thinkers, well versed in the ethics and safety issues of living and learning in a digital world, then you want them to be blogging. If developing your students' ability to communicate effectively with other students, adults, and experts from around the world is important, then they should be blogging. If you want your students to be able to tap into the networked information and learning environments available online 24/7, then they should be blogging. In other words, all of your students should be blogging.

What Makes Blogging Great?

Even if you have little experience with blogs, you probably know that they involve writing. And if all that blogs were good for was motivating students to write more and to be more thoughtful, thorough editors—*that alone* would be enough to recommend blogging in the classroom.

But blogging involves so much more. Blogs are published to the world. The world is invited to start a conversation about each blog post and give feedback, encouraging the blogger to read the blogs of the commenters and give them feedback in return. So blogging involves writing, but also reading. Blogging can be used in every curricular area. Students can explain their learning, thinking, or understanding in math or reading or social studies or science—or any curriculum area or topic you can think of. Students can comment on current events, write creative pieces, letters, and poetry. The list is endless.

The upshot is that your students should be blogging.

There are two main ideas you will read about repeatedly in this book.

1. Blogging is not an "add-on."

2. Blogging involves becoming part of an online community that must be respected as such.

These ideas are both so important to the understanding of blogging in the classroom that they come up often in our discussions of using the tool. So let's start with a brief discussion here.

Most of us in education are faced with continually growing curricula. We are constantly asked to teach more and more, prepare for more and more tests, and cover more and more content without anything being taken away. The reasons for this are simple—the world is expanding in its content; therefore, more content must be taught in order for our children to be ready to succeed. Additionally, we are faced with an ever increasing number of dropouts and nonliterate adults. Governments, in an effort to change this situation, turn to assessment as a tool to assure a better education for all. This translates to more assessments being handed to educators, which means more time spent preparing students for these specific tests.

Test preparation time plus ever more content equals less time for "extras." That is why it is important for you to understand and embrace the idea that blogging is not just one more "add-on." We will show you many ways to change the way you think about working within and assessing your curriculum and to incorporate blogging into what you're already doing.

The second idea, that blogging involves becoming part of an online community that is to be respected at all times, is a valuable principle for us to embrace in the 21st century. More and more of our future contact with others will take place online. When our students graduate, they will most likely enter vocations where contact with others online, nearby and across the world, is a regular part of their days. We must teach children how to use online tools to help them be successful in the future.

As responsible educators, we often worry about safety issues when it comes to students being online. And safety is very important. In a later chapter, we will discuss specific safety rules we cover in our classes. But beyond the safety issue is the issue of good digital citizenship—we want our students to learn to be respectful, considerate, and specific in language when participating in life online. These are skills we often teach for students dealing with each other within classrooms. Now it is time to make the person on the other end of a blog real for our students, so they understand that respect and responsibility reach past the walls of the classroom and pertain to any other people they might come into contact with, whether face to face or online. So throughout this book, you will find lesson ideas and content emphasizing respectful contact among students.

We hope that this book will help you begin to make a change in your classroom. We can no longer sit by, waiting for the administration or government to tell us how and when to use educational technology. We can make changes one classroom at a time. And blogging is a tool that can help us move toward that change. It is an engaging educational communication tool that easily spans subject areas and is useful for all ages. The fact that you are reading a book about blogging shows that you are open to changing learning tools you and your students use and willing to change how learning in your classroom happens. Welcome to blogging and to a wonderful new world of education for the world as it is now and will be in the future.

1

How Blogging Relates to Standards

A blog is in many ways a continuing conversation.

—ANDREW SULLIVAN, AUTHOR, EDITOR, POLITICAL COMMENTATOR, AND BLOGGER

As we look at reading and writing standards from countries around the world, we see that we all require the same basic skills from our students. Students have to be able to read and interpret information from a variety of texts and to communicate effectively with a range of audiences, from teachers, to classmates, to people in living in other parts of the world.

Blogging can help students practice all of these essential skills. Let's see how.

Basic Skills

If we start with basic writing skills, we see that students first need to be able to "adjust their use of spoken, written, and visual language (e.g., conventions, style, vocabulary) to communicate effectively with a variety of audiences and for different purposes" (National Council of Teachers of English/International Reading Association Standard 4, www.ncte.org/standards). When blogging, students should have two main goals. One is to write a blog that others will *want* to read. And the second is to *communicate* through comments on other blogs. Both of these goals require adjustment of the written language in order to communicate effectively. While students blog, they must work hard to make their writing interesting to the reader. After all, the more interesting it is, the more readers they will attract. And the more readers they attract, the more comments they will receive. For children, this functions like a popularity contest. They want "friends," so they work hard to change their writing style to suit their audiences. The students get what they want, and we, as educators, end up with students who actually work at adding voice and style to their work. We see, year after year, an improvement in the quality of writing not only from the usual students motivated by grades, but by so many who become motivated by doing well for their audience and the improvement they see in their own writing skills.

Engaging Others

As educators, we also want students to "engage in conversation in pairs and small groups on familiar and topical issues" (Ireland Standards: National Council for Curriculum and Assessment English Syllabus, www.ncca.ie/uploadedfiles/Junior%20Cycle%20Review/English_guide(1).pdf). Blogging, by its nature, just happens to be perfect at fostering this behavior. Let's take a look at Joe.

Authentic Interests and Authentic Audiences

Joe is writing yet another blog post about something that interests him: his favorite sports team. He is motivated to write, interested in his topic, and working toward writing for his audience. Many of his classmates start to read the blog. Some agree wholeheartedly with his posts, while others adamantly disagree. His comments start to grow. When we look at some of the comments, we see that the students are very respectfully giving their opinions about how this team has been playing all season.

We also notice that Sonia feels so strongly about this topic that she writes her own blog post about it. She has stated this in her comment and linked back to her own blog. Now, Sonia happens to have a strong following in a class across the country. So when her post gets read by her audience, many of these students link back to Joe's original post. Soon there are dozens of students around the world writing about their favorite sports teams. They are being respectful and considerate of each other, linking back and forth. They are having amazing conversations on familiar and topical issues.

~~~~

Was writing about a sports team an assignment handed out by Joe's teacher? Actually, no! But motivated by authentic interests and an authentic audience, he and other students are writing and certainly meeting writing standards. We have seen this situation occur many times. Sometimes it does begin with an assignment, other times, not. But children do love to communicate about topics that interest them. And with some specific lessons teaching them how, they can be very successful at it.

Respecting Diversity

Another skill central to education is one where students are taught to "develop an understanding of and respect for diversity in language use, patterns, and dialects across cultures, ethnic groups, geographic regions, and social roles" (NCTE/IRA Standard 9, www.ncte.org/standards). "Accomplished teachers understand that their students may belong to communities that speak a diverse range of dialects and languages other than English" (Australia Standards: Standards for Teachers of English Language and Literacy in Australia, www.stella.org.au/index.php?id=8).

Technology is shrinking our world at a phenomenal rate. We can no longer expect that our students will graduate from school and communicate only with people in their own small community. We must teach students to be global members of society. Blogging is an integral part of this goal. As we will show later, it is quite easy to connect with other blogging classes around the world. The students will have many opportunities to communicate with others from many different countries, ethnic groups, economic areas, and geographic regions.

We have found that even simple exchanges between two students can do wonders to improve respect for diversity. One example is the child from New York who blogged about dinner. A typical dinner for this Indian child was rice and beans eaten by hand. The comments poured in, asking questions about using silverware, explaining how dinner worked in other households, commenting that rice and beans is a pretty common dinner for many cultures. What began as a simple blog about everyday life became a lesson in diversity and respect for children from around the world. And no educator could have planned it any better.

Effective Communication

Of course, we want students to use proper language skills. Students need to be able to write clearly, appropriately, and effectively (England Standards, Key Concept 1.1, Competence: http://curriculum.qcda.gov.uk/uploads/QCA-07-3332-pEnglish3_tcm8-399.pdf). Blogging almost *demands* that students learn to be better editors of their work. Once students are blogging and develop an audience, they become more concerned about how their audience perceives them. This naturally leads to students being more motivated to edit. And when they see another blog that isn't edited well, it gives them insights into how their own posts are perceived. Many students have come to us, showing us a blog post that was poorly written. This allows a teaching opportunity for two important lessons. One lesson promotes tolerance and respect. We do not comment on posts with suggestions to improve them unless that was specifically asked for. The other lesson is one regarding audience reaction: "Imagine what other people might be saying about your blog, if this is how you feel about someone else's blog. Remember this when it is time to edit your own blog." Now, when we cover editing skills in class, we can easily refer back to the need for editing our blog posts. Students now have a vested interest in learning the skills. We often observe students requesting editing help from teachers, support staff, and their peers. They begin to build a network to assist them in their learning because they discern value in producing quality work. We have accomplished our goal!

Blogging also covers interpreting text in content area classes. "Pupils should be taught the technical and specialist vocabulary of subjects and how to use and spell these words. They should also be taught to use the patterns of language vital to understanding and expression in different subjects. These include the construction of sentences, paragraphs and texts that are often used in a subject" (England Standards, National Curriculum Use of Language/Reading: http://curriculum. qcda.gov.uk/key-stages-3-and-4/general-teaching-requirements/use-of-language/ index.aspx).

In the United States, Common Core Standards have recently been adopted in English language arts. These Common Core Standards expect that "students should demonstrate increasing sophistication in all aspects of language use, from vocabulary and syntax to the development and organization of ideas, and they should address increasingly demanding content and sources" (Common Core State Standards Initiative, ELA Writing: www.corestandards.org). As we've shown, blogging will give students the motivation to improve their writing.

Of course, blogging also assists students with educational technology skills. Many of the ISTE National Education Technology Standards for Students (NETS•S) are covered through blogging. Creativity and Innovation are clearly defined within blogging. Students learn and are motivated to be more creative each time they blog in order to receive more comments. Distance communication is key in blogging. By carrying on a conversation through blogs, comments, and embedded media, students learn to "communicate information and ideas effectively to multiple audiences using a variety of media and formats" (NETS•S 2b; see Appendix C). Digital Citizenship (NETS•S 5) works well with Internet Etiquette (see Chapter 3 and Appendix C).

When we use blogging as a way for students to demonstrate their understanding of content, we are giving them opportunities to practice using vocabulary they will encounter in content area texts. Imagine giving your students a blogging assignment after completing a hands-on science experiment in class. Ask your students to explain the experiment and the outcome. Ask them to explain what the outcome would be if a variable were changed. Perhaps they can blog about why the experiment didn't work as anticipated. Maybe they can talk about how they will change the experiment to achieve a different outcome. You not only get a clear idea of who understood the day's lesson and who didn't, but the students are given the opportunity to practice all of their writing skills and the chance to utilize the vocabulary of the class. By watching the discussions that occur in the comments, you can then see how your students react to questions about the lesson. This can occur in science, social studies, math, foreign language—any subject. And because blogging allows you to connect easily, imagine doing the same experiment or project along with other classrooms around the world, sharing their experiences and perceptions with your students. The possibilities and ramifications are compelling.

A blog can also be a place for students to document their research on a specific topic. Imagine having a student blog daily about a research project. Each day we see what she has learned and accomplished. Her teacher gets a daily update on her work. This gives the teacher an opportunity to steer her in a different direction or to send her some specific links to helpful sites. It gives other students an opportunity to learn the subject along with her and see how others research topics. At the end, she can embed a link to her project in a post for all to see. Chapter 7 contains many more content area ideas.

As you can see, blogging in the classroom is much more than a chronological order of posts. It is a valuable instructional tool for reading and writing, a perfect place to practice new content area vocabulary and skills, and a venue for communication among students and teachers, students, and class to class.

2

Changes in Pedagogy

There is nothing wrong with change, if it is in the right direction.

—WINSTON CHURCHILL

We have already touched on how blogging can be part of a changed pedagogy that prepares our students to communicate effectively and is rich in the learning and thinking opportunities it offers in virtually every subject. In this chapter we will focus on the specific pedagogic changes that must occur to maximize blogging's educational impact and why these changes are necessary.

Let's explore how a blog could be used to help enhance instruction in several typical subject area scenarios.

Blogging and Language Arts, Math, Science, and Social Studies

Blogging and Language Arts

In a fifth grade classroom, the students begin the day with reading. They are learning about fantasy and reading a book within this genre. Worksheets are handed out, on which students list realism and fantasy examples from their book. They keep character lists and write descriptions. Those students with writing disabilities often struggle with this assignment and might not complete it at all. Organization is an issue for everyone, as some students lose their papers and must start over each day.

In a separate fifth grade classroom, the class is also studying the fantasy genre, but they are using their blogs for various assignments. One student, Sam, keeps a list of characters on his blog, with others adding information about the characters as comments to the original post. Another student, Rachel, keeps the list of realism and fantasy examples, with others adding to the list via comments. What is different about using blogging for this assignment instead of printed worksheets? Once the lists are posted to the blogs, the world begins to notice and take part. Students in another fifth grade class across the country are reading the same book. They add to the lists. Jack decides to keep a summary of the book on his blog, along with his commentary. Kim, from a different class, decides to do the same, but she disagrees with Jack, who really doesn't like the characters in the book. Jack and Kim begin a series of blog posts and comments back and forth, discussing the effectiveness of the author's decisions relating to character traits. Finally, the classes finish the book and watch a movie based on the story. Each child then writes a blog post comparing the book and movie. There are so many different opinions about which was better—the book or the movie—that both classes continue the discussions long after they have completed the book and the teachers have moved on.

~~~~

Blogging and Mathematics

Now it is time for math. The class is beginning to learn long division. This is a difficult skill for many of the students to master, so the teacher, understanding the need for multiple avenues of instruction, has provided various websites with games for practice. Some of the students post reviews of these websites on their blogs. The teacher has also enlisted some of the stronger students to create screencasts—movies demonstrating the steps—and embed the screencasts within their blog posts. One student, Lucy, made a mistake during her screencast and corrected herself within the movie. She decided to leave her mistake and correction in the movie. What kind of comments did she receive?

While many students commented about her method for solving the problem, most comments were about how brave she was for making an error and demonstrating that. Along comes Dylan, a fifth grader from a different class who is always afraid to raise his hand for fear of being wrong. He bravely decides to create a screencast of his own with a different math problem. He struggles with the understanding, getting assistance from his teacher, and then posts this video on his blog, dedicating it to Lucy. The classes go wild with comments back and forth about the bravery of both students. All the students become motivated to work hard in math class so they can create their own videos.

~~~~

Blogging and Science

Today's science lesson is an experiment using simple machines. The previous week, the students were all asked to pose a hypothesis about the experiment they are performing today. They wrote up their experiments on their blogs. For the whole week, students have been reading and responding to each other's ideas, pointing out inconsistencies, suggesting changes, but also being supportive and positive because the teacher has taken the time to teach the students how and why it is crucial to have civil, supportive discourse when commenting in blog communities. Science teachers from around the world have also entered the conversations with helpful links and suggestions for videos.

Today, while the experiments are being performed, the teacher walks around with a video camera, recording as much as possible. Guess where this video will go? That's right—on the blog! Now the students get to evaluate their hypotheses based on the lesson. Prior to blogging, the writing of science lessons stayed in the classroom. Websites and videos were limited to those that the classroom teacher was familiar with. Thanks to this blog, other experts chimed in, students became more analytical about their thinking, lively dialogue ensued, and the learning went further than expected.

~~~~

Blogging and Social Studies

In social studies, the class is studying slavery in the 1800s. The students are given the assignment to write a letter as a slave owner discussing the ramifications of the end of slavery. This letter will be written using specific vocabulary and historic content. Each letter is posted to the class blog, with an explanation of the assignment. Comments start coming in from other countries that also have dealt with slavery issues, including children in countries from which slaves were taken. Those children discuss the slavery issue from a completely different point of view. Other children comment about similarities with their own countries. And one child comments about slavery that exists today. These fifth graders have not only learned about slavery from a United States point of view, but now have many perspectives regarding slavery around the world. A simple history lesson has turned into much more.

~~~~

Blogging's Educational Impact

Does every lesson have to end in a blog post? No. Can it? Yes, but as with any tool, the more that it is used the same way each time, the more mundane it becomes. So watch for that. You might notice that within these four examples, the blogs were used in four different ways: as a book discussion, as a video venue, as a science journal, and as a letter. By changing the assignments, teachers keep blogging fresh. Students begin to see the possibilities of using their blogs as a portfolio for other types of work, instead of just as a writing notebook. There are so many tools that can be used to further communication in a classroom. Blogging is just one. And many other tools can be embedded into a blog. Each student's site can become a portfolio for the year's work—easily shared with classmates, teachers, parents, and grandparents. How great is that?

And did you notice blogging isn't just about writing? A blog post can simply be a link to a podcast where students share their thinking orally. An embedded drawing or series of drawings or other artwork might be a student's reaction to a story or explanation of a science concept or an event from history. An embedded YouTube video might show a student's understanding of a particular novel. Think how these possibilities facilitate differentiating instruction for students.

We often hear about incorporating higher-order thinking skills into lessons and assignments. Just recalling information and having a general understanding aren't enough. Perhaps you noted how much of the learning associated with blogging involves those higher-order skills?

- Blogging about learning

- Defending a blog post through comments

- Creating a video, podcast, or artwork to represent learning and then discussing it

Writing, discussing, and debating about blog posts cause students to analyze and think deeply about what they've learned so they can take a defensible position or explain their thoughts. As with any difficult skill, the more guided practice you experience, the more skillful you become. As students blog, they are practicing and honing these crucial skills. Respectful discourse lessons are learned as students deal with making or arguing a point without coming off as being demeaning or derogatory.

A hugely positive change in pedagogy that occurs when students blog is the move from short response and fill-in-the-blank answers to the deeper thinking that goes into sharing their reasoning with the world. Students realize that teachers, students, parents, and others are actually going to read their posts. That realization changes how answers are approached. Again, blogging doesn't make that happen instantly, but as students experience what happens, and with you as their guide to make sure they understand the ramifications, it does happen. Blogging allows continuing practice in these difficult but immensely powerful deep thinking skills.

Pedagogical Changes

A blogging classroom does not happen by chance and does not get created in one day. The important thing to understand is the changes you must go through in pedagogy in order to incorporate blogging effectively into your classroom. So let's take a look at some changes that need to be made.

Be prepared to spend more time on analyzing text, ideas, and learning.

- Spending less time on answering questions from a workbook or worksheet will give you more time for higher level ideas.

- Try to integrate curriculum. This will allow you to cover all your requirements in less time. For example, combine your history lessons with your reading lessons, reading historical fiction or nonfiction books relating to your history lessons.

Begin to move to a paperless classroom.

- Do not recreate the worksheets on a blog. Instead, consider assignments that will lead naturally to a conversation with others. For example: Replace the worksheet of comprehension questions about a chapter in the book with an assignment asking students to draw a picture of their favorite scene. Post the pictures on the blog with the excerpt from the book and have comments compare the excerpt to the picture. You will easily see who understood the story, the students will be more motivated to focus while reading, and the commenters will practice giving suggestions respectfully.

- In blog posts, have students keep lists of vocabulary words they find in the book and explain how they connect to these words. The commenters will add their own connections, building on vocabulary, while discussing the book.

- Instead of recreating a math worksheet with multiple problems, have students create a video showing how different students solve one problem and embed it in a post. Students can then compare the different methods used to solve the same problem.

Build in time for rewriting and editing.

- For blogging to improve students' writing, they must be given the opportunity to revise their work to fit their audience. This skill is one they will naturally want to master as comments come in about their blogs.

- You may decide to have one 30-minute period a day for students to revise their blog work with assistance from you or their classmates.

- You may decide to give them the revision time for homework.

- You may give them a date for submitting blog posts early. Should they submit the post two days before the due date, you will give suggestions for improvement. This puts the responsibility back on them.

Let go of other methods of teaching in order to fit blogging into the day.

- Blogging is not an add-on to the learning. It is the learning. Use blogging to check for understanding, expand thinking, and connect ideas.

- Have students work out science hypotheses in their blogs, encouraging them to comment with suggestions to each other.

- Have students discuss, within the blogs, essential questions relating to your social studies topic.

Technology integration has been slow to take hold in schools for a number of reasons, but one of the biggest roadblocks to effective integration has always been that technology is viewed by teachers and administrators as an addition to everything we are trying to cram into the curriculum. Many school technology initiatives have gone by the wayside, mainly because the technology was used to do schoolwork the same as always.

Technology is valuable in that it opens up new ways to learn—ways that match up with 21st-century life, thinking, and skills. When thinking about blogging, you must realize that this is an effective, powerful tool that will help prepare students for their futures. Blogging is one way students will learn to communicate with others. It is also a powerful tool for assessing students' understanding and communication skills. Blogging should become part of the everyday activities of the classroom.

Being able to express oneself effectively has always been a difficult and important skill that has been given far too little focus. When you begin to have students blog their discussions with others, one issue that will inevitably be noted is how inarticulate and assumptive they often are (at first) when expressing their opinions, thoughts, and ideas. Students are generally inexperienced at having effective oral discussions of this kind and rarely have had thoughtful, ongoing written discussions. This will be new to most, and so taking the time to teach students how to express themselves effectively and then giving them many opportunities to practice becomes crucial. Because today it is so much easier to be connected— learning, connecting, and publishing globally—we have entered a new era when communicating effectively, clearly, and concisely has never been more critical. Blogging sets the stage and provides multiple opportunities for students to practice being competent, articulate communicators. Take full advantage!

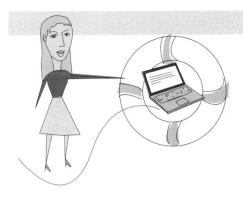

3

Before You Start: Internet Safety and Etiquette

*I never had a policy; I have just tried
to do my very best each and every day.*

—ABRAHAM LINCOLN

Unlike Abraham Lincoln, we do need
policies in school. And as you might suspect,
policies are necessary around blogging in
the classroom.

Imagine doing an animal collage with your students. You ask for magazines to be brought into school for this collage. You collect magazines for a week prior to the assignment and, as the students bring them in, they pile in front of the room. During your free time, you go through the magazines to make sure they are appropriate for school. If you have parents who are doctors, ask them to send in some medical magazines. Those are out—too many pictures of naked people. *National Geographic* is popular. The problem with those is that in addition to many fabulous animal pictures and pictures of habitats, there are also pictures of people who are less than fully clothed. Then there are the monthly women's magazines: *Redbook, Ladies' Home Journal*, and so on. These, too, have appropriate pictures for your project but are full of ads for bras and panties.

What to do? You could begin by going through each and every page of the hundred or so magazines, pulling out the pages that are inappropriate. Or, you could eliminate the ones that were mostly inappropriate (medical magazines, some of the *National Geographics, Cosmopolitan*) and teach the students what to do with the rest. So you choose the latter. After all, the children are viewing these magazines at home, anyway. You might as well teach them how to deal with it.

So you have a lesson on what students should do if they come across an inappropriate picture. Should they tear it out of the magazine and walk around, showing it to classmates? No. Should they yell out to everyone to come see what they found? No. Should they calmly turn the page? Yes. And, as long as you stay calm about this subject, so will your students. Yes, there is always that child who wants to pause on the inappropriate content a bit too long. But, with vigilance on your part, you are able to use these tools and have a successful lesson creating animal collages.

Now let's look at the digital-age classroom. It is still time to do animal research, but now we are finding pictures online and pasting them into a blog we are creating about animals. We will also be using the pictures for a digital story about our topic. Instead of using magazines, we are using the Internet for research. This is a place where we can find amazing sites about animals with wonderful pictures. And we can also find some wildly inappropriate sites with naked people, underwear, and surgery being performed live. So how do we allow students to use the Internet, maintain some control over what they are finding, and make the activity a positive learning experience? Much the same way we sifted through the pile of magazines in our initial example. We create lists of acceptable sites for students to use, we do our best to filter obviously inappropriate sites, we teach students what to do if they come across something inappropriate in their search, and we are vigilant while they are working.

Internet Etiquette: What's Expected?

You have made the decision to begin blogging with your class. This means that your students will have access to the Internet in all its wonder and openness. But before you set up student blogs, before you give the students an assignment, before you unleash your class onto the World Wide Web, there are some important areas to cover.

Signed Permissions and AUPs

First and foremost, you must get parental permission for your students to use the Internet and post their work. You want your students' parents to support what you are doing in the classroom. This means being totally transparent with your intentions. Your school or district might already have a standard permission slip for parents to sign. Examples of permission forms appear in Appendix A.

Check to make sure that the permissions enable your students to search the Internet and post written work, pictures, audio, and video of themselves. Some districts still only ask for permission for pictures. This is not enough anymore. Let parents know that their children will be posting their writing and will be communicating with other students and teachers around the world. Let them know that their children will be surfing the Internet, looking for important data for research or using online tools in order to enhance their work. Give parents every opportunity to ask questions, see examples of what is out there, and be reassured that you will be teaching their children about Internet safety and etiquette (or *netiquette*).

In some classrooms, permission is granted for each specific item the children will be posting. So parents indicate specific, separate permissions for schoolwork, pictures, audio, video, communication with others, and Internet use. Some parents give permission for some items and not others. If you hand out permission slips right before Meet the Teacher night, then during parent visits you can explain the permission slip and show many examples of how you will be using various tools, moderating what the students are doing online, and covering all safety issues.

Remember to be honest. Inform parents: "Is it possible for your child to come across something not so appropriate? Yes. Is it possible at home for them to do the same? Yes. How do we handle it in school? Let me show you the system we have in place and the rules we set up in class." When you focus on the content and educational uses, parents are much more likely to allow their children to use the Internet for learning. Interestingly enough, it is the students themselves who become the biggest advocates for posting work online. When children are not allowed to be in a class video or participate in a Skype call with another class, they often go home and explain again to their parents what the class was doing and why they should be allowed to participate. Updated permission slips often arrive shortly after the first online experience.

Once the permission slips have been returned, it is time for your AUP. An AUP (acceptable use policy or authorization of use policy) is basically a contract you will have with your students and parents. It clearly lays out all the details of what students can and cannot do online. What are your expectations for your students when they are online? Do you want them to be allowed to check email in school? Should they be allowed to search freely for data, or do you want to limit where they can go? Do you want to let your students go online at any time, or should they ask your permission first? What would you like your students to do if they come across something inappropriate online? Should they notify you? Shut down the window? These are decisions you need to make up front, and they also should be reflected in your classroom setup. In our rooms, we allow students to use the Internet as needed. They are taught to shut down windows and notify us quietly of inappropriate sites. This works well for us. You might want to set tighter restrictions on your students. There is an example of an AUP in Appendix A (Form A-1) of this book.

You should note that both the permission slips and the AUP for our classes are updated each year. As more technology and applications are utilized by students and integrated into daily classwork, more transparency is needed for parents and more expectations are set up for students. Don't feel you have to get it all perfect the first year. Try to anticipate all you will be covering, but don't worry if you miss something. Just keep a note to add it in the following year. You many also find that you want a separate permission slip for a specific project. For example, when our students worked on the Harris Burdick Writing Project, we were Skyping individually with students across the country. We were also exchanging blogging URLs and communicating in Google Docs. Because we had never had such close communications with a specific class before, we sent out letters outlining the project, explaining how it related to our curriculum, and asking parents to sign the letter, indicating that they knew what we would be doing. This was not a requirement in our school or district, and we could have continued without this extra notice. But we find that transparency is the best way to prevent misunderstandings later on. And, by that point in the year, the parents were comfortable with our use of technology and were excited by the project, not nervous about it.

Transparency is most important when using technology. Your students will feel comfortable with all the new tools, but many parents will not. By keeping everything open, you can ease their concerns. Make it clear how you handle breaking the rules, demonstrate the educational use of tools, give examples of lessons taught about safety and netiquette. In one classroom, the teacher often uses YouTube for posting class videos and for grabbing educational videos for students to watch. She first had to acknowledge to the parents and the administration that there are some wildly inappropriate videos on YouTube. She then showed a variety of educational videos, while also demonstrating how she used the embed code to place those videos on her own blog. This allowed students to view the videos without actually going to the YouTube site. Because the teacher was being honest and transparent, parents were more comfortable with the use of this site. In fact, many parents created their own YouTube accounts at home in order to maximize the learning there.

Teaching Respect, Acceptance, and Responsibility

Naturally, before you ask students to sign the AUP, you must clearly define your areas of concern with your students. Because we feel it is very important for children to demonstrate respect for others both on and offline, we spend time in September reading books relating to acceptance. Appendix B lists picture books, novels, and nonfiction books that are suitable classroom conversation starters relating to acceptance of others.

In our class, we discuss and teach lessons about respect and responsibility. We are very clear about the fact that respect and responsibility carry into Internet interactions. Children often don't think about the fact that there is a real person on the other end of the computer connection. They often feel that they are invisible and anonymous on their end and can, therefore, get away with anything. It is important for them to learn that all Internet-connected computers have an IP address, so what is done can be traced back to the original user. It is more important for them to understand that there is a living, feeling human being on the other end. The comments they leave on blogs must be respectful at all times. Their conversations in chat rooms and on videoconferencing sites should be respectful. If your students and parents sign an AUP as part of registration, go over a copy with students and remind them that they signed it, agreeing to its terms. Then decide on the consequences of breaking the contract. Does a student get a warning? Or is there a no tolerance policy for breaking the rules?

Internet Safety

In addition to covering respect and tolerance for others, you should include cyber safety lessons. There are many terrific online sites that cover such topics as what information is appropriate to post, what information should be kept private, how to handle the situation when a stranger starts to talk with you, and what to do when you click on a link that brings you to an inappropriate site. There have been times when our own students have come across ads or sites that have inappropriate content. When this happens, our rule says the student should immediately close the window and notify the teacher.

The teacher needs to be notified for a variety of reasons. One is to be able to explain to concerned parents and administrators exactly what was on the page. Another is to find out why and how the students ended up on the site. If they were there on purpose, then the AUP rules were broken and consequences follow. If they were there due to a poor search, then a lesson in proper search methods would be helpful. Maybe they ended up on the site because something about the site was tagged inappropriately. This has occurred in my class, most often when students are searching for pictures. We use a picture site that has a safe search option, and the safe search option usually works. But sometimes a wildly inappropriate picture shows up under safe search. When this occurs, I contact the site and let them know about the picture. It is usually fixed rather quickly.

Internet Safety Sites

The following links will direct you to sites discussing online safety:

Carnegie Library of Pittsburgh Online Internet Safety Resources for Parents (and Educators)
www.carnegielibrary.org/research/parentseducators/parents/netsafety/websites.html

YouTube: Beware of Friends Online (Video: 3:02 min)
www.youtube.com/watch?v=393Mab4z95E

Cyber Safety for Children
www.cybersafety.ca.gov

Cyber-Safety
www.cyber-safety.com

Basic Internet Safety for Kids
www.staysafeonline.org/in-the-home/basic-internet-safety-kids

Cybersafety for Kids Online (A Parent's Guide)
www.ncpc.org/cms-upload/ncpc/File/chcyber.pdf

Wired Kids
www.wiredkids.org/wiredkids_org.html

Teaching Cyber Safety and Internet Etiquette

Following are guidelines for teaching Internet safety and netiquette: Begin with an AUP and teach safety, proper search techniques, and privacy issues. Teach online etiquette and work on it in the classroom.

Begin with an AUP.

- Go over to the AUP in class.

- Make the rules of Internet use clear to your students.

- Discuss the specific consequences of breaking rules.

Teach safety.

- What should students do if they come across an inappropriate site?

- What should students do if a stranger comes onto a site and begins chatting with them?

- What information can be shared online?

Teach proper search techniques.

- Help students narrow down topics to avoid inappropriate sites.

- Show students sites you have set up for them to assist in searching.

Teach about privacy issues on the computer.

- Children do not understand that texting, emails, and instant message (IM) chats are not private. Therefore, they think that speaking poorly about a classmate in a text to another friend is fine. They don't realize that the other friend has the power to forward that text to everyone else in his/her contact list. What is written online is public and might as well be printed on the front page of the newspaper. This is a powerful message for children to understand.

Work on etiquette.

- Children usually do not understand that there is a feeling human being on the other end of their comments. They need to follow the same respect rules online as they would in the classroom.

Once I had students who had found a link they wanted to include in a blog about their favorite amusement park. They came to me with a worry. "Teacher, there is a link we want to include, but there is an advertisement on the site that we don't think is proper for our blog." I went to take a look. There was a sidebar advertisement for a lingerie store. The ad did change periodically, but we decided together that, no, it would not be appropriate to link to that particular page on their blog. Instead, we found a different link about the amusement park that did not advertise anything but the amusement park. And I praised the students for being so conscientious about the ads on the site. There was no mad rush to the computer to see the lingerie ads. In fact, none of the other students were aware that this situation was occurring. The students had enough training to know how to handle inappropriate content.

A teacher friend had her students do research on the Middle Ages, and several students were looking for facts about the kings and queens of the era. Their search came across a page with a photo of scantily clad women. The teacher noticed a commotion at that computer, and soon the whole group approached her and told her what they had come across. The teacher asked what they had done, and they replied, "We hit the back button right away and got off that page!" The teacher explained that they had done just what she had taught them to do and was pleased that they had let her know what happened. She then asked them how they had searched for their information and helped them narrow their search so that wouldn't happen again. The next day she taught a mini-lesson for the whole class and used the experience to teach them how to make their searching on the net safer and more efficient. Two of the students' parents happened to stop by the room after school, and their kids explained what happened. At first the parents were concerned, but when the teacher questioned the students in front of their parents about how it happened and what they did about it, the parents completely changed their attitude and were pleased their children had learned how to be safe and appropriate online.

Once again, we must remember that transparency is the key to good parental relations. We find that when you let parents know that you are teaching their children what to do if something inappropriate comes up, they really appreciate it and don't overreact the very few times something does happen. But, if you haven't mentioned to them what could happen, and that you are teaching their children safe use and what to do when something inappropriate happens, that is when you have very upset parents who want to pull the plug on Internet tools.

Teaching students about possible issues and educating them and their parents about safe use is so important. Schools and teachers are experts at doing this— for example, think of the bus safety, fire safety, and "stranger danger" classes we teach. Scissors, sharp pencils, compasses, playground equipment, driving to school in a car or bus—all can cause injuries. But all of these things are deemed too valuable to do without, so we teach safe use and monitor students. Accidents and misuse happen sometimes, and we deal with those instances and sometimes have to re-stress adherence to safe use. The Internet and online applications such as blogs are extremely valuable and powerful tools, so we must teach ethical, safe use; monitor their use; and re-stress safe use if an issue arises. Children won't learn proper, ethical use without experience.

One really great blog lesson that gets assigned annually by many middle grade teachers is the Seven Random Facts Blog Post. The students are asked to create a blog post that tells seven random facts about themselves. In addition to practicing writing skills, this is a terrific way to teach students about information that is appropriate to share online and information that should never be shared. For example, a child can say one fact is he or she lives in the suburbs on Long Island, but the child cannot say "in the suburbs in the small town of New Hyde Park near the duck pond." This gives too many clues as to the child's exact location and is, therefore, not appropriate to share.

Once the posts are completed, students are then directed to find other classes participating in this assignment and comment on the facts that are very similar or very different from their own. The teachers can link to the other classes' blogs from their teacher sites to make the blogs easier for the students to find. The students would have to read many blogs to find just the right ones to comment on—respectfully, of course.

The reality is that cyber safety and netiquette should be covered all year throughout your lessons. Take advantage of teachable moments that arise during class.

4

So Many Choices

The indispensable first step to getting the things you want out of life is this: decide what you want.

—BEN STEIN

Decisions. Decisions. Decisions. You have decided to blog; you are in the process of teaching your students about Internet safety and etiquette. It is finally time to set up your blog(s). Now come all the decisions.

Which Blogging Platform Will You Use?

The first decision you need to make is which blogging platform you will use. There are many different blogging platforms to choose from that are appropriate for classrooms. Some are specifically designed for educators, and some are designed for any blogger. They all have pros and cons. Some teachers start with one platform and then move to a different platform when they find one that better suits their needs. Don't worry that once you choose one, you are stuck with it. Try it out and see if it is a good fit for you and your students. Another way to narrow down the choices is to talk to blogging teachers about what platform they use, why they use it, and would they recommend it. You can sometimes find their email addresses—if not, just leave a comment with your contact information on their class blog.

Common Educator Blogging Platforms

We suggest taking some time to peruse the following class blog platforms. These are some of the more popular blogging platforms to get you started. Note what other educators are using. This is only a small sampling of blogging platforms that are available for educators. There are many out there, and you should experiment until you find the one that fits your needs.

Class Blogmeister
www.classblogmeister.com

> This free site, created by David Warlick specifically for educators, is a "walled garden" for blogging. (See "Walled Garden" Blogs on page 37.) You need a code for your school in order to participate. You then have a variety of options—keeping it password protected, opening it up to the world, or moderating all or none or anything in between. All blogs and comments get approved by the teacher before being posted. The teacher has a main blog, and all students' blog pages run off the main teacher page.

> ***Support:*** Class Blogmeister has a large support system in place for assistance and troubleshooting. There is a Yahoo group you can join off the main page. This group is a place where you can find other users, get questions answered, and connect with other classes. In fact, this is where the two authors connected and started collaborating with our classes.

Blogger

www.blogger.com/start

This free site run by Google is a very public site. You do have options of moderating comments or not. Each student has his/her own blog. You can have access to each blog, as Blogger allows for multiple authors. All blogs and comments are approved by either student or teacher prior to posting. Note— Blogger does have a "Next Blog" button on the top of each blog. This button brings readers to another Blogger site, not necessarily related to education.

Support: Blogger has an official Blogger Help Center where you can find FAQs or get answers through email. This is a Google help area, so there are no people to connect with here.

Edublogs

http://edublogs.org

This site, created for educators, allows for complete control or complete freedom. Students have their own blogs, which teachers have access to. All comments can be moderated, allowing both students and teachers access to approval. There is an option to make all comments moderated by just the teacher. This site is either free with ads or, for a fee, ads can be removed and control handed over to the teacher.

Support: Sue Waters is the Edublogger. She blogs about ideas for using Edublogs, as well as lends support for connecting with other bloggers and tackling technology issues. You can access her blog off the main Edublogs page.

KidBlog

http://kidblog.org

This new free blogging site, created for educators, is another walled garden for blogging. Teachers have total control over blogs and comments.

Support: While KidBlog offers email assistance for support, at the time of this writing, this was a fairly new site. Therefore, groups had not yet formed around support or collaboration with KidBlogs.

21Classes
www.21classes.com/shop/product

> This free blog site, created for educators, is yet another walled garden for blogging. The teacher has the main blog with student blogs linked off the main page. Control is in the teacher's hands, although there are options to give students more control as time and skills progress.
>
> *Support:* 21Classes has a FAQ page for both teachers and students. There is also email support available.

Your Class Blog: Public or Private?

Once you have chosen your blogging platform, it's time for the next decision. Do you want to make your class's blog public or private? With any platform, you have the choice to keep your blog private (just visible to you and your class), make it public (visible to everyone on the Internet), or password-protect it (visible only to those you choose to allow in).

Some teachers choose to make their class blogs private. Perhaps their administration or parents won't support or allow student work to be public, or the teachers are still uncomfortable with having their students' work available online. For this type of teacher, a private blog is a great choice. Some teachers begin with the blog private as the teacher and students get the hang of how blogging works, and then open the blog up when they are comfortable, which usually happens much more quickly than the teacher assumed.

Some teachers prefer to keep the blog password protected. This allows the teacher and administration to decide who can read and participate in the blog. Students, parents, fellow teachers, and collaborative classrooms would receive the password to be allowed into the blog. No one else would have access. This is a nice middle ground for teachers who are not yet comfortable with going public but would like to invite select individuals in. It is also more comforting to administrators and parents just getting used to the idea of having children work online.

Some teachers are ready to go! They choose to make their blogs public, allowing any other classroom, teacher, student, or interested Internet user access to the blog. Should this be your choice, you might want to consider carefully moderating comments (see To Moderate or Not to Moderate?).

Regardless of your choice, just remember that a huge part of the excitement and motivation of blogging is that it *is* public—your students can get comments from, communicate with, and make connections with others and learn how to be safe online. This opportunity is lost when the blog is kept private.

To Moderate or Not to Moderate?

Your next decision will be about moderation of blog posts and of comments. To moderate a blog means to check each post and/or comment prior to publishing it online. All blogs have the option of moderating comments. Most "walled garden" blogs give the option to moderate blog posts, too.

In moderation, there are two items to consider. One is about the blogs themselves. Do you want to moderate blog posts before they are published? Should you decide to moderate, it likely means that all moderation will be done by you, the teacher. The students will submit posts, and you will decide whether to publish them. This allows you time to help students better edit their work, add more details to ideas, and correct misinformation—all before posting to the Internet. If you choose to moderate blog posts, you must check the blog frequently for new posts waiting to be published. You and only you are responsible for what shows up on the blog. You can assure parents and administrators that you are monitoring the site carefully and nothing will be posted that is inappropriate. This type of blog is especially recommended for younger students.

> **"Walled Garden" Blogs**
>
> A *walled garden* blog
>
> - limits membership to approved users
> - limits access to approved users and visitors
> - typically gives the option to moderate

Perhaps you would like to give your students the freedom to post blogs as desired. This frees you from having to check so often to see if posts are waiting for your approval. It allows students to be timely with their assigned postings instead of relying on you to get the assignment posted on time. You could use comments to correct any misinformation the student might have included. This type of blog is recommended for older students who are capable of taking necessary safety precautions when publishing their work on the Internet. You will need to remind them often of the AUP they signed.

Once you decide about blog post moderation, you need to decide about comment moderation. On almost any blogging platform, you will have the ability to moderate comments. This is highly recommended for a classroom blog. Should your blog be visible to the world, you never know what kinds of comments might come in. Sometimes, comments are spam—promoting online businesses. These do not belong on a classroom blog. Sometimes comments are disrespectful, talking mostly about the problems with the blog or just stirring up trouble. You would likely choose not to have those comments displayed on the student's post. Sometimes the comments that come from other students aren't completely appropriate. We talk more about teaching your students to comment appropriately in Chapter 8.

Should you decide to moderate comments, you will need to check the blog frequently for incoming comments. This gives you an opportunity to connect with some of the commenters about their choice of words, especially if they are from your own classroom. It also gives you the opportunity to check any URLs that are included in the comments before they end up online. Some are inappropriate. Some are just broken links. Comment moderation allows you yet another way to reassure your administrators and parents that you are maintaining control over what shows up on the blog.

Should you decide to allow comments through without moderation, you must be prepared to check each blog frequently in order to remove any inappropriate comments as soon as possible. All posts and comments can always be removed by the blog administrator (you) even after they are posted online.

You also might want to allow your students to moderate their own comments. This means students approve all comments before they are posted, eliminating inappropriate material. In this case, your students are seeing everything first, so you will need to be clear about informing parents and getting their approval. For older students, allowing them to moderate comments might be a good choice. It is an important skill they need to learn: to be timely and careful in their moderation. For younger students, we recommend you keep control. They are working hard to learn the skills involved in blogging and making comments. They are not really ready to make decisions yet about whether or not a comment should be approved.

Who Will Control the Look of the Blog?

For some students, the look of the blog is very important. They can spend hours changing the background, redoing fonts and font colors, and adding cool widgets (fun little applications that can be added to blogs; see Embeds and Widgets). For others, the content of the blog is what is important. Some blogging platforms are set up so all changes in appearance have to be approved by the teacher, and some platforms are left open for the students to design.

Once again, you have to decide how much control you want to give your students. I have some students who would like to spend most of their time finding gaming widgets to add to the site. While they are learning skills about searching for widgets and grabbing code to embed in the blog, they are not practicing blogging or writing skills. But I do find some value even in this, as long as you help students find a balance. Students with "fun" blogs tend to get more comments on those blogs and are, therefore, making more connections with other students. So I usually allow them to post what they want as long as they also keep up with any assignments required by me. As a rule, I do not spend time in class teaching students how to find widgets and/or change the look of their blogs. There are always students in the class who learn on their own and spend time teaching the others.

Embeds and Widgets

Explore some of the following tools that are often used in conjunction with blogging.

Voki
www.voki.com

> Voki allows students to create an avatar and have the avatar speak. They can record their blogs and/or record comments about blogs. They can also record any information they wish to share with their readers. This tool is perfect for hesitant writers and visually impaired students.

VoiceThread
http://voicethread.com

> VoiceThread is a collaborative tool that allows pages to be made with either pictures or video. Then the world can comment on each page.

Video Sites: YouTube, TeacherTube, SchoolTube

www.youtube.com
http://teachertube.com
www.schooltube.com

YouTube, TeacherTube, and SchoolTube are among various video sites that allow you and your students to grab embed codes and embed a video into the blog. Students can find coordinating videos for their subject matter. They can also create their own videos, post them on a video site, and embed the video into their blogsites, where others can comment on their videos.

Picture Sites: Compfight, FlickrCC

http://compfight.com
http://flickrcc.net
http://flickrcc.bluemountains.net

Compfight and FlickrCC sites such as flickrcc.bluemountains.net allow students to find pictures with a Creative Commons attribution. As long as they cite their sources, students can include the pictures with their blogs, adding an extra layer to their work.

ClustrMaps

www.clustrmaps.com

ClustrMaps is a map site that allows you to register your blog and grab an embed code for adding the map to your site. The map visually shows how many people visit your blog and where they come from. This is a very powerful motivation for blogging, as the students see their audience growing.

Wordle

www.wordle.net

Wordle is a word cloud creator that allows students to take the text from a blog, post it into the site, and create a word cloud. This allows them to see a graphic display of words they use too often, or ideas that come up a lot in their writing. A copy of the wordle can then be posted into the blog.

Animoto

http://animoto.com

Animoto is a site that allows you and your students to import pictures, choose music, add text, and create a movie. The embed code easily allows you to put this video on your blog.

How Will Students Choose Passwords and Blog Names?

Each student will have to choose a blog "handle" (nickname) and a password, or you can make them up and assign them. Here is a great opportunity to add a safety lesson about online handles and passwords that relates to any online work your students ever do—not just blogs. Many of our students are shocked to learn that passwords should not be birthdays, addresses, pet names, or phone numbers. They think these are fairly private. Take this time to teach about using safe passwords and keeping passwords private. For younger children, we highly recommend keeping a list of passwords somewhere safe, in case the students forget them (and some will). Some blogging platforms require the teacher to input the passwords.

When choosing a blog handle, first remember that there is a law in effect that provides guidelines in this area. The Children's Online Privacy Protection Act (COPPA, www.ftc.gov/ogc/coppa1.htm) does not allow children younger than age 13 to post personal information, including first and last names online (first names alone are okay). So for younger children, blog handles should never include a first and last name. Many students use hobbies or favorite sports teams with a student number given to them in class. They look like YankeeFan3, DogLover9, or Reader12. The number allows you to figure out who they are quickly, and the name allows other students to know a little more about each child.

Give Up Control Gradually

The choices you make when starting your blog are important but not written in stone. Should you decide to moderate all blogs, for example, and then realize later that you want your students to post without your approval first, just change that option. Don't get so bogged down by the decision you make that you end up making no decisions. If you are really stuck, begin by keeping everything within your control. Then you can gradually give control back to the students as you and they feel more comfortable blogging.

5

How Do You Blog? Step by Step

*The vision must be followed
by the venture.*

—VANCE HAVNER,
AUTHOR AND EVANGELIST

In order to get your students into blogging, you have to have some idea of how to blog yourself. So our suggestion is to take a look at a few blogging platforms and try one or two of them out. Go through the management part of the blog. See if you can understand the basic steps in managing a blog. Read some existing blogs, and leave some comments so you learn how that works. Notice what various bloggers put on the sidebars of their blogs.

All blogs have three main parts involved in basic blogging: the article box, the comment section, and the management pages. Let's start with the article box. This is where a blog post is written. The settings on all article boxes are pretty similar. They tend to function like a word processing document. You can change fonts, font sizes, and font colors. You can usually insert images and links. Sometimes, there is a feature that allows you to add video easily. Usually, however, you need to embed an HTML code to add video (this is fairly simple). We will show some examples in this chapter.

Let's walk through the basics of publishing a text post to a blog. This is what you and your students will start with. Images, video, and other content can come a little later, when you are ready for them. As we stated earlier, different blogging platforms often function in similar ways, so we will use Class Blogmeister to demonstrate the step-by-step procedure, using screenshots of actual pages. This whole process takes only a few minutes but will look like more here because we are showing you every step.

Before You Post

Prior to creating a blog post, you must create a blog account. For most blogging platforms, this is fairly easy and instantaneous. It usually is just a matter of registering your name and email address. Sometimes, like in Blogger and Edublogs, you will need to come up with a blog name during registration, so be prepared to be creative.

Class Blogmeister, our favorite class blogging platform, is a bit different. You first need a school passcode to register your class. In order to get a passcode, you must first email David Warlick, the creator of Class Blogmeister. When you are on the Class Blogmeister home page, you can scroll to the bottom and find a link to email Class Blogmeister. Once you click on that link, it brings you to an email form. Fill it out with a comment that you are a classroom teacher and wish to get a school passcode. You must wait for him to respond, but the response time is usually pretty short. Be sure to check with your school district IT person first. Your school might already have a passcode.

Once you have a passcode, you simply click on the register button on the Class Blogmeister home page, and you will be able to register your class.

Writing and Publishing a Blog Post

First, log into your class blog from the login page. In Class Blogmeister you type your login name and password in the blanks under "To Edit Your Blog" in the right-hand column. Note that "Zample" has typed in his name and password.

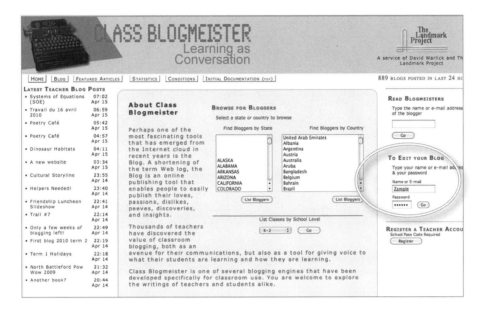

Once you have logged in, you come to the Edit Mode page. In Class Blogmeister this page is basically the same for the teacher or the student; the only difference is that the teacher page has more choices of things to do. Click on "Articles" at the top of the page to write a post.

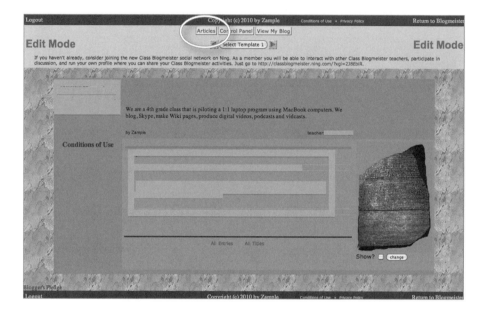

Once you or your students have clicked on the "Articles" button, you will come to this window. Note the buttons at the top right labeled "Text" and "Graphical."

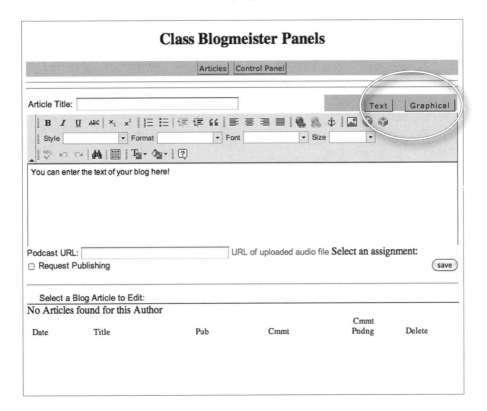

Click on "Graphical," and the window will appear as shown. Note that many parts resemble what you see on a typical word processing page. The first step in creating your blog is to type in the title of your blog post in the box labeled "Article Title."

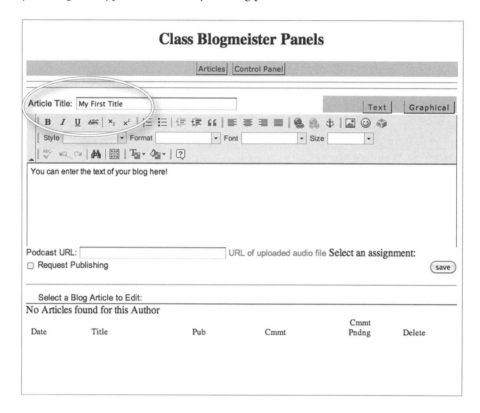

The blog post itself is added to the text box. Text can be typed in directly or cut and pasted from another document. Students often type their posts into a word processor so they can save them to finish later in case they don't get done. When finished, they cut and paste their posts into the text box.

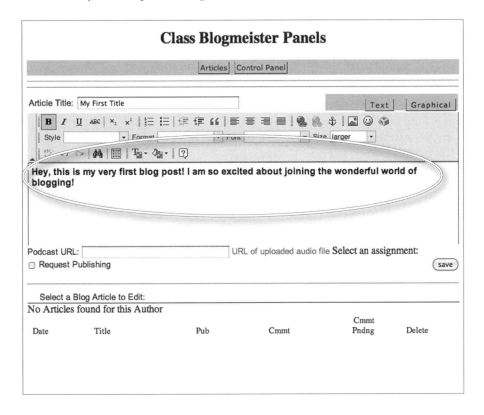

When the post is ready to be published, the blogger requests publishing by checking the "Request Publishing" box.

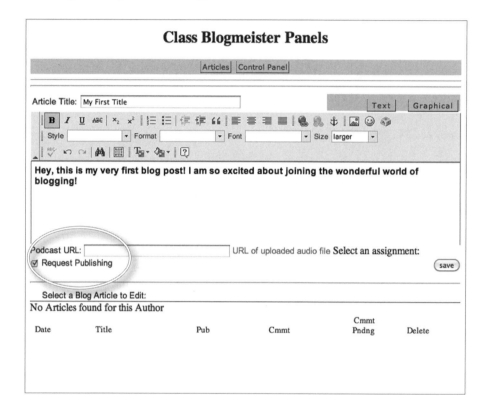

Next, click the "Save" button on the lower right, and depending on the settings you've chosen, the post is either published right away or sent to be moderated (approved) by the teacher, who can publish it if satisfied with it. The teacher can even make some edits before it is published. Our blogs are set to be moderated by the teacher, so the post won't show up until the teacher approves it.

Once the "Save" button has been clicked, the title and post seem to disappear, and the title shows up at the bottom of the window along with the date of publishing.

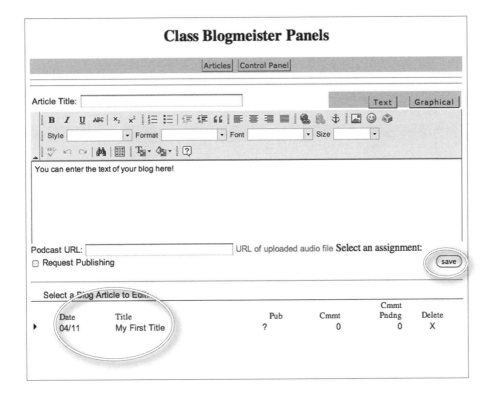

This is how your student's published post looks. Now when others go to the student blogsite, they can see the post and add comments. See how easy it is to publish a blog post?

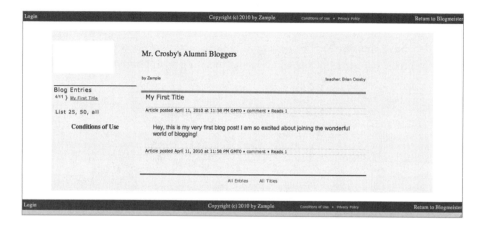

Here is an example of a text box from Blogger, another widely used blogging platform. Note the many similarities in functionality between Blogger and Class Blogmeister.

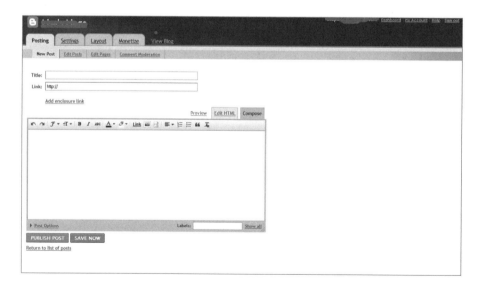

Making a Comment on a Blog Post

Once you have written and published some posts, you are ready to leave comments.

Find the link labeled with the word "comment"—it is usually a different color. In Class Blogmeister there are two comment links, one at the top of the post and one at the bottom. Different blog platforms have the comment links in different places and may only have one, but they are usually easy to locate. You have read this post and decided to leave the writer a comment. So click on either comment link.

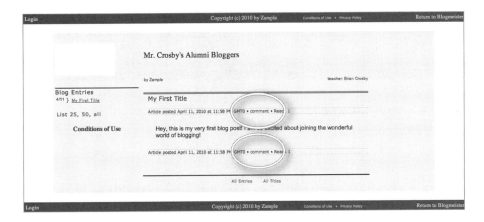

When you click on the comment link, you come to this page. If there were other comments already left, you could read them where the words "Posted Comments" appear at the bottom. Since you are the first commenter, there are no other comments yet. Click on the "Add a Comment" button.

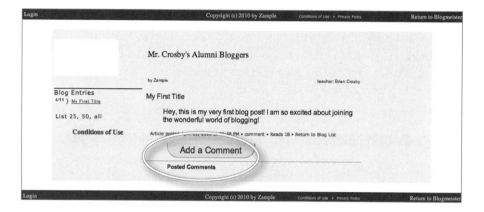

Now you come to the comments page. Note that you can reference the blogger's post at the top in case you forget what was said.

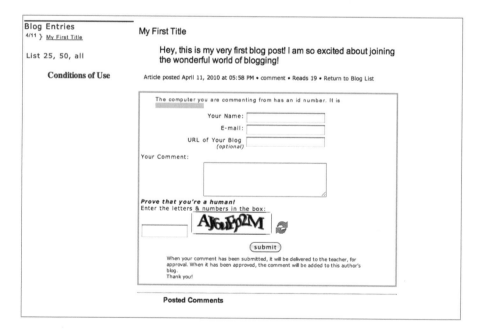

To post a comment, the first step is to type in your name in the "Your Name" box. Remind students to use their blogging handle or first name only here (see Chapter 3 for more on Internet safety and protecting student identities). There is a place for an email address.

Using Email in Class

There are many sites that require email to access them. Additionally, an email address may be required when your students leave comments on blog posts. If your students all have email addresses, then you are good to go. But if your students do not have email addresses, there are some work-arounds:

- Create an email account for your whole class. Each student will access a site using the same email address and password. Benefits: The students can help each other remember the email address and password needed to access a site. You have to invite only one email address into the site, instead of one per student. The drawback to this is that when you are looking at the posting history of a site to see which students added work, the names will be the same for all the students.

  We use this method when work is being done in class with a teacher monitoring.

- Send home a letter requesting an email address for each child. The letter should include the reason it is required. Talk about the tools you will be using. Include some parental advice; for example, parents should be monitoring the email that comes in.

  This method works well for older students. Most already have email addresses and are ready to go.

- Google Apps for Educators allows educators to create accounts for each student. The students have individual logins and passwords, but all mail comes to the teacher. This tool is free but requires a domain name. Speak with your IT person to see if you can get one.

  This method works well for students when they are not able to have their own accounts but need a separate identity within sites.

In Class Blogmeister, you can leave the email address blank unless your students have email addresses that you want them to be able to share. Some sites, such as Edublogs, require an email address. For this, you can have students use a class email address provided by the teacher.

Filling the next box, "URL of Your Blog" (see top of page 57), is optional, but it is an important box that you do not want to leave blank. Some blogsites, such as Blogger, allow the commenter to leave a comment anonymously. Do not allow students to do so. This is how the person receiving the comment finds the blog of the commenter. The idea is to make it easy to find your blog. By filling in your blog address here, you ensure that the comments you leave become links back to your blog. A major part of blogging, remember, is having readers. This is one of the best ways to make others aware of your blog. You left them a comment, and it is typical that they will at least check your blog out and maybe leave you a comment as well. The reason this field is optional is that you don't *have to* have your own blog to leave a comment. You do have a blog, so leave your blog address. Start this habit with students right away so it becomes part of what they do automatically when they leave a comment.

Next, write your comment. You can type it directly in the "Your Comment" box or write it in a word processor and cut and paste it here. If the comment gets long, it's a good idea to compose it in a word processor first. There is usually no spell check in comment functionality, and if this is not your own class blog, there is no taking the comment back to edit later, so use that as motivation for students to be thorough editors.

To avoid comment spammers, you are asked to prove you are human. The letters and numbers you are asked to enter (called a "captcha") are purposely skewed to make them impossible to be read by a spammer's scanning software. Type the code into the box provided. It is case sensitive, so capitalize or don't, as shown in the code, or it will not work. Students sometimes struggle a bit deciphering these codes themselves, so warn them ahead of time that if it doesn't work, they may have missed a character or typed it incorrectly. It doesn't take long for students to get the hang of these codes. When finished, click "Submit." As long as the captcha was entered correctly, your comment is sent. Remember, most student blogs are moderated, so the comment may not show up until the teacher sees it and allows it to post.

Here is a comment ready to be submitted. Click the "Submit" button when you're ready.

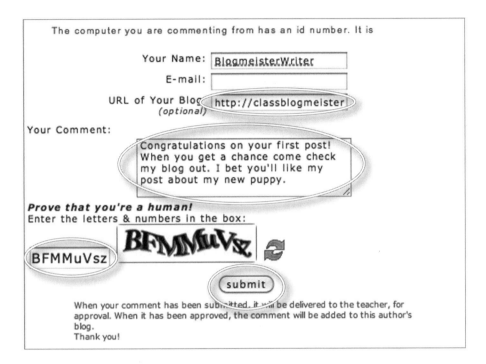

After you click "Submit," this window appears.

Congratulations! You have now written and published a blog post and commented on the post.

Moderating Comments

When your class is first starting to comment, having them comment on your own class blog for practice is a good idea. If you set the blog up so you can moderate comments, you'll be able to see all these first attempts at commenting and can point out any issues that arise. In Blogmeister, when you open the "Approval Tool" and click on the comment, it opens a window like the one pictured. If the comment is appropriate, all you do is click the "✔ Approve" link at the bottom.

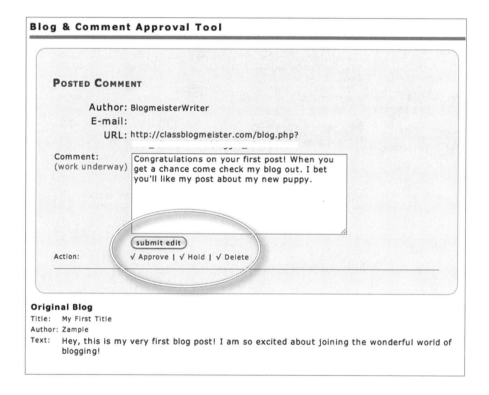

When students leave comments on other blogs, you will not see the comments before they are published. Consider how you want to handle this. You can create a rule that your students must allow you to review their comments before they submit them. You can also have them comment only on other classroom blogs where you have an agreement with the other teacher. This way, that teacher will feel free to let you know if a student is commenting inappropriately.

After you approve it, the comment appears on the student's blog post.

Here is the comment page from Blogger. You can see it has the option for posting anonymously. Remember, you don't want students leaving anonymous comments. That stifles conversation and negates much of the educational value of blogging as a conversation.

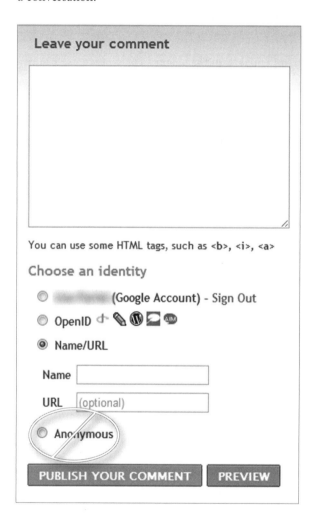

This comment box is from Edublogs. You can see that the email address is required. Your students will come across comment boxes that are different from time to time. They are usually easy to figure out.

Embed Codes (HTML)

As you and your students visit other blogs, you will notice that some posts contain artwork, photos, videos, podcasts, and other media. How did they do that? They use embed codes. *Embed* means to incorporate a piece of media within the body of a post. It's actually a lot easier than it might sound.

In order to add embed codes into your blog post, you first need to find something to embed. YouTube videos, Vokis, VoiceThreads, and podcasts all have associated embed codes.

Embedding a Photo to a Post

Here is a photo from the Flickr photo-sharing site. After you choose the photo size, Flickr provides the HTML code. Simply highlight and then copy the code that is in the box. You do not need to understand HTML coding in order to use these codes.

Change license?

To link to this photo on other websites you can either:

1. Copy and paste this HTML into your webpage:

```
<a href="http://www.flickr.com/photos/36362146@N02/4119936441/"
title="DSC06272 by crosbyclass, on Flickr"><img
src="http://farm3.static.flickr.com
/2611/4119936441_b4ff9aa203_m.jpg" width="180" height="240"
alt="DSC06272" /></a>
```

Here is our post from earlier. Notice that the "Text" button has been clicked, and that has changed the look of the window. It doesn't look as much like a word processor anymore, and the post we made before is also showing the HTML code that makes it work (the code is contained in the angle brackets). Don't worry, the coding appeared by itself; you don't have to put it there. You are now ready to add the embed code you copied from the Flickr site.

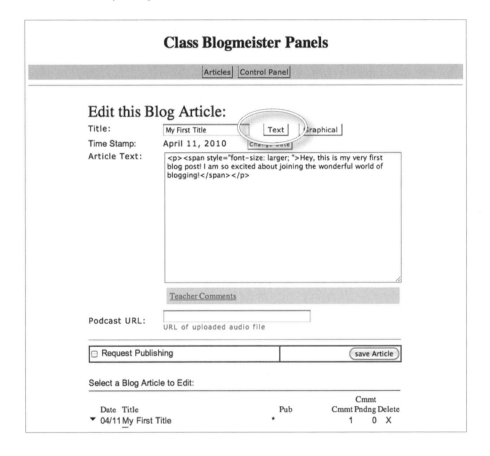

Paste the HTML code copied from the Flickr photo page into the text box, click the "Request Publishing" box, and then click on the "save Article" button.

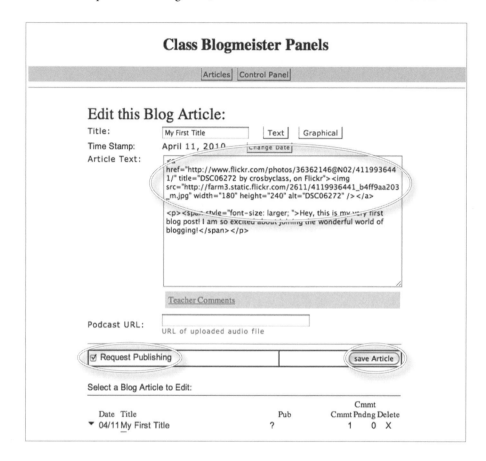

Your blog post is now illustrated!

Embedding a Video to a Post

To add a YouTube video to a post, the steps are much the same:

1. Find the video you want to embed.

2. Click the "Share" button.

3. Copy the embed code.

Embed codes make it easy to add media and widgets to your blog posts or to your main blog page.

When adding embed codes in the Blogger platform when writing a post, you will see a tab that says, "Edit HTML." When you click on that tab, you will see the HTML coding. Add your code there.

Recommended Video Tutorials

There are many, many video tutorials available on YouTube for every blogging platform. With a little searching, you'll find exactly what you need!

How to Add an Image to a Blog—Class Blogmeister
by Rob Jacklin
www.youtube.com/watch?v=ueMOA35pnug&feature=related

Class Blogmeister Introduction
by David Warlick
www.youtube.com/watch?v=1pfesOfnIOE

Class Blogmeister Initial Setup
by David Warlick
www.youtube.com/watch?v=al9aBUTx4_g

How to Create a Blog on Blogger—Setup
www.youtube.com/user/BloggerHelp

Page Management

The final part of blogging that you need to understand is page management. To access your management pages, you will need to log in to your blogsite. The management pages vary from site to site, but most have many of the same features. You will see the blog posts that are pending (waiting for your approval), the comments that are pending, and the posts that have been published. You will also see the layout section. This allows you to create the look you want for your blog. Some blogs have very limited layouts. Some are more elaborate. Most allow you at least to choose a background color.

epbyStep**Chapter5**

This is the teacher's management page for Class Blogmeister. Each student gets listed here, along with all the posts by that student. There is also a delete button next to each post. This is one place to manage pending blogs and comments. By clicking on the blog post title, you open the article box, allowing for editing and adding suggestions for the student.

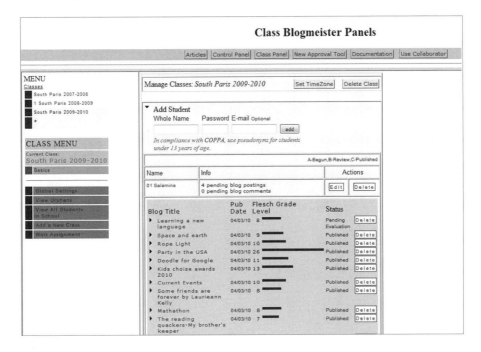

In Class Blogmeister, this is what you'll see when you click on the title of a pending blog post. The post itself is in the left box. The right box is for teacher suggestions to improve the post. Once suggestions are typed there, the student can access the suggestions by logging in and clicking on his/her article. The suggestions do not get posted onto the site. Once the post meets with your approval, you would click the "Publish?" box to publish the student's blog. (Students do not publish their work directly. When they click the "Publish?" box, their work goes to you for review.)

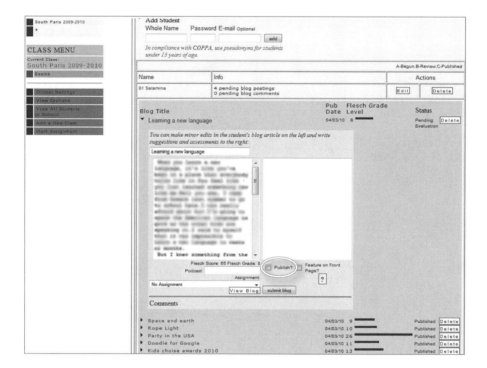

This is the front page of a class blogsite in Class Blogmeister. The main teacher blog is in the middle. On the right side are all student blogs. Each name is linked to the individual student pages. The left sidebar has related links inserted by the teacher. There the class can find other class blogs to access. The background color, sidebars, and corner images were chosen in the management pages. And you can change things anytime. Start with a simple look if you want, and as you gain experience with other blogs you can come back and use those ideas. The individual student blogs have many of the same options.

6

Managing Blogging in the Classroom

This time, like all times, is a very good one,
if we but know what to do with it.

—RALPH WALDO EMERSON

"Let's do this!" was pretty much our
thinking when our classes first started blogging. We were so excited. We had everything
set. But then reality set in. How do I manage
all of this? How do I get my students onto
the computer? How do I assist all of them at
the same time? What if I want this to be a
homework assignment?

Of course, before you get them blogging, you do need to teach your students how to use the blogging platform you have chosen. Show them how to log on to the site. Show them how to post articles and comments. Show them how to check back to see if you have added any suggestions. Each platform has different methods of posting, so learn yours before you introduce blogging to the students.

Finding Time to Blog

You also need to know if there is a time limit to keeping a blog post page opened in edit mode. For example, in Class Blogmeister, students get logged out after about 20 minutes. For sites such as this, your students would be better off creating and editing posts in a word processing program first. This way, they can take their time, take advantage of the editing tools in the word processing program, and not have to worry about losing what they've done. You might also recommend frequent saves while writing, just in case the computer program crashes in the middle of the class. A good idea for students who often lose files would be to have them work in a cloud program such as Google Docs, where the word processing file is stored online. All the student has to do is remember the login. Using Google Docs, students can access their work on any computer, anywhere there is Internet service.

Now the question is, "How do you get all your students on the computer to post blog articles?" If you are lucky enough to be in a 1-to-1 classroom (one laptop for each student), then you don't have to worry about management. All of your students will be on their laptops at the same time. There are various strategies that teachers use to see who needs help and who doesn't in this situation. Signs next to the computers work well for this. One side says, "I'm fine"; the other says, "I need some help." This way you can easily see who needs support. You might also have a "See three before me" rule: students must ask three classmates for assistance before relying on the teacher.

But most of us are not in a 1-to-1 situation. So what do we do? One option might be to sign up for your school computer lab or pull the "roving" laptop cart into your room. In either of these situations, you would want your students already to have gone through the writing process on paper and have an edited copy of their posts ready to type, so you make the most of the time they have access to computers. If, like at many schools, lab time is only once a week for

30 to 45 minutes, posts will preferably be kept to a length allowing students to get them posted in that period of time (although stretching an assignment over several weeks is something to consider, too). Should you be limited to this 30- to 45-minute time and have only a few students who cannot complete the assignment in that allotted time frame, then consider putting those students on the classroom computer or a library computer to finish up. You don't want to return the following week to the lab, have a new assignment, but have a couple of students still working on the first assignment. And for those students who finish early, a perfect follow-up assignment is to read others' blog posts and comment on them.

Another possibility is having students post from home. Some classrooms have good access at school with many students having limited access at home, so blogs can rarely be given as a homework assignment. However, many teachers have an opposite situation. So it might be easier to have your students post from home. They can do all or much of the writing at school, then type and post it as part of their homework or do the entire assignment as homework.

Perhaps in your situation there are several computers in your classroom. Then you could create a station or center that students rotate through during the course of the week. You could also work out with other teachers a plan to have several of your students visit their rooms to use their computers to post from. If you plan it well, you can manage to have every student working at the same time by using the computers in five different classrooms and the school library. You would, of course, have to roam during the work time and monitor student progress. Other times you might get about half of the class on computers this way. Consider teaching a lesson to the students left in class and then rotating the groups and re-teaching the lesson to the other group.

Think of other computers your students might have access to in your unique situation. What can you do to make this work? Get your students involved. They may be aware of resources you are not and might be part of the solution. In fact, students get so involved in blogging that they often write posts on their blog on their own anytime they want, on any subject they want. They could use the public library computers, computers their parents have access to at work, and those in other students' or friends' homes.

Finding Time to Moderate

How many times have you started something, only to find it took up so much time you swore you would never try it again? I think all of us have been in this situation. Teachers have many time obstacles to overcome during the day. Our curricular requirements seem to increase each year, standardized testing takes up a great deal of time, and we are lucky if we get to work in our classrooms during a prep instead of having a meeting. That is, if we have a prep at all. So with all these time constraints, how do you find the time to moderate one blog, much less a whole classroom full of blogs?

Tips to Making Moderating Simple and Efficient

Some teachers choose to moderate one day a week. Some choose once per day for comments and once per week for posts. Some use the students' class blogging time to moderate the blogsite.

- Moderating should not be something you do all day, every day.

- Set a time for moderating comments and moderating posts and inform the students of the time(s).

Make it clear to the students when you will be moderating both comments and blog posts. You need to try out different scenarios until you find what works best for you. Here are some examples:

1. Mrs. A checks for blog comments each day. She feels that she wants to get comments onto the site as quickly as possible to motivate the students to keep writing. After each assignment, Mrs. A gives herself three days to check blog posts. This gives her time to edit, make suggestions, and grade the blogs. Once she has made suggestions, she gives the students one day to fix up their posts before resubmitting. She checks blogs during preps and at home after school hours. This used to be the time she would sit with papers, marking them up and scoring them.

2. Mr. B checks for posts and comments every day during his prep time. He feels it is important to respond quickly to each student in order to encourage continued writing. This does take him some time, but he feels it is time worth spending.

3. Ms. C checks for comments each day. She, like Mrs. A and Mr. B, feels comments need to go up to keep the motivation level high. Comments take very little time to check, so she spends about 10 to 15 minutes per day on them. For posts, she takes longer. While her students are blogging in class, Ms. C sits at her computer and checks what comes in. She tells students to spend some time reading and commenting on other blogs, which are linked to her site, while they await her suggestions. As each blog is checked, she lets the blogger know that it is time to revise the writing. This 45-minute period every other day gives her plenty of time to work with students on their writing.

4. Mr. D does not have access to computers often in school, so his students work on paper. Once blog posts are completed, he uses writing time to meet with them individually to edit and revise their work. Students revise their work on paper. Then, once a week, he takes the students to the lab and has them post their edited, revised work. At this point, checking for posts takes very little time. He has already seen their work and really just needs to check to see that they are typed properly. This is work he completes at home and during preps.

There are many strategies for managing your time. The important thing to remember is that blogging should not be all-consuming. If you are spending more time moderating blogs than you would marking papers, then you need to try another method. We find that the time we spend moderating posts and comments is equal to or less than the time spent marking papers. Remember, this is not an add-on. Blogging is replacing other work we no longer do, such as using worksheets to evaluate learning. It shouldn't take you any longer to check blogs than it did to correct other work.

On to
Classroom
Blogging

*Blogging is best learned by blogging ...
and by reading other bloggers.*

—George Siemens

Like your first time doing any new lesson or project, you might be both a bit nervous and excited at this point. Go with that. It's probably one of the reasons you became a teacher. While deciding on your first assignment, keep in mind that what will be created throughout the year is a portfolio of thoughts and ideas, as well as samples of writing. So decide which direction you would like the blog to go. If you are an English teacher, you might want to align the blog assignments with your novels. Perhaps your first assignment should be a review of a favorite book.

If you are a math teacher, you might want your blog to be explanations of problems solved. So your first assignment could be a Problem of the Day. If you are an elementary teacher who teaches all subjects, you might want your blog to be a reflection of the students' learning throughout the year. So the first post might be goals for the year.

Getting Started

Some of us are required to obtain a short writing sample from our students at the start of the year. To more or less guarantee that all students will be able to think of something to write about, we offer several topics: What is the most exciting thing that has ever happened to you, someone in your family, or a friend? What is the best gift you ever received or gave someone? What is the scariest thing that ever happened to you? We spend some upfront time brainstorming so that all students are able to think of something to write about. These become not only baseline writing samples, but could be their first blog posts, too.

If you'd like a short piece to post for the students' first experience, poetry might be a good start. You can have students write poetry about any topic and then post their poems. If students have more than one poem, which is often the case when you are writing poetry, they can even publish several as separate posts, giving them practice in posting to their blogs. You will note that some students who pick up on the simple steps of posting right away can then help others.

Sometimes your first time blogging won't be at the beginning of the school year. If that is the case, then students could write about blogging for the first time and their excitement and feelings about that. Additionally, later in the year, the class has had some common experiences that might be good writing topics. A recent field trip or science experiment or responses to books they've read or projects or themes they've participated in are great. Any other memorable experiences would work. If your students have previously completed writing assignments, you can have them post those to get right to the mechanics of posting to their blogs.

Blog Post Ideas

Here are some examples of "first of the year" blog post ideas for students:

Example 1: Last week we began writing our Hopes and Dreams for the new school year. Now it is time for you to publish your first blog post about your Hopes and Dreams. Go into your page, post the article in the article section, click the Post button, and wait for the teacher to approve your blog. Be sure to check back to see if comments were made by the teacher for more editing.

Here is your teacher's Hopes and Dreams post for you to use as a model:

> My Hopes and Dreams for this year center around creating projects, from which you can learn. I not only enjoy working on projects but I enjoy watching you learn, grow, and get excited about coming to school. I read a book this summer called *Reinventing Project-Based Learning*. I got some exciting new ideas from this book. I look forward to using these new ideas to create amazing educational projects for the year.

Example 2: In your first blog post, write a brief description of the most exciting or most memorable thing that happened to you over the summer.

Example 3: You will write a response to the video, "Future Fright," viewed in class today. What were the issues the Gordon family faced upon arriving in the United States after their stay in another country? Describe how your life would change if you lived in a country with a government that did not support individual rights.

Example 4: I hope you all had a fabulous summer vacation and that you are all rested and ready to work hard—and of course have fun. For your first blog assignment, I want you to choose one of the following options to write about.

a. Write about one thing that you did over the summer holidays. It can be a funny story, crazy adventure, and/or a fun activity that you participated in.

b. 3–2–1: Write 3 things about yourself, 2 things about your family, and 1 question that you have about the upcoming year.

Notice that in these examples, the assignments are simply stated and modeled. This first blog post should simply be practice for the students, giving them an opportunity to learn how to publish a post, check for teacher suggestions, and receive comments. As we move further into the year, the students will be instructed to pay more attention to writing traits, editing skills, and specific content area information.

Setting Expectations

Once your blog assignment is posted, you will present the assignment in class. Here is your opportunity to lay down your expectations for completing assignments.

- Do you have a due date?
- Do you want the students to write following specific writing rules (introductory paragraph, body paragraph, concluding paragraph)?
- Do you want them to write in a notebook first, revising and editing before posting?
- Do you want them to type in a word processing document first to take advantage of the editing tools of the software?
- Will this assignment be started in class and finished at home?
- Will it all be done in class over the course of a few days or a week?
- Will it be a homework assignment?

You need to be specific at this time so you can set the stage for the rest of the year, although we do find that we start simply and add more specifics as we move into each assignment. See Chapter 6 for logistical information about classroom management and using school computers.

First Blog

We would recommend completing the first blog post in class. Although you might want future blog assignments to be completed at home, using class time for this first one allows students to get the support they need for the technical aspects of blogging. For example, in our favorite venue, Class Blogmeister, students get timed out of the blog editing page after 20 minutes. So they need frequent reminders to copy their work so they can paste it back in if they should work beyond 20 minutes. Students also need to learn how to log in to their site, how to submit posts for approval, how to check for teacher suggestions, and how to resubmit revised blogs. All of this can be done in class during the first blog writing. And, if you record your instructions (on your interactive whiteboard or in a screencast program) while you go through them with the students, you can post those recordings for students' future reference, saving yourself much reteaching time.

Notice the reaction of students as their first posts publish to the world. Notice your reaction, too. As students post, have them check out their classmates' blogs, and that will garner other reactions. The fun and learning have only just started!

Content Area Blogging

Blogging can be a useful tool in every subject area. This section of the book separates blog ideas into different content areas. We hope you will find these to be helpful and inspirational, regardless of the subject you teach.

Reading/Language Arts

Language arts lends itself perfectly to blogging. After all, blogging is ultimately about reading, writing, and communicating. Some specific ideas for your class might include the following:

- Have your students write a summary and review of a book they are reading.

- Have them make written plot predictions halfway through books.

- Direct them to write stories in the style of a picture book you just read to them.

- Some books lend themselves well to writing the next chapter after the end of the book. What might the characters do next, based on what students have learned about them from reading the book? Students should be challenged not to deviate much, if at all, from established character traits. Students could even blog a description or outline of what could happen in the next chapter and then read and comment on others' posts.

- Post a rough draft of a piece of writing, and ask for constructive criticism from your audience. Later, post the final copy.

- Find another class or classes that are reading the same story or book as your class or group in your class. Students can post about anything you choose for their focus skill about the story or book you are reading, main idea, characters, predictions about what will happen next, and so on. Now have your students read and comment on others' blog posts. Have them look for others who agree with their point of view and then those who disagree, and have them leave comments about what they agree with and disagree with and why. Have them try to make their case, well enough to perhaps change another blogger's mind to their point of view, even a little, with their respectful arguments.

- Post a story, underline specific words you would like to change to make them more descriptive, and ask for suggestions. You could ask for descriptive phrases that paint a picture of the event in your mind, too. Then use some of the ideas and explain why you chose them, and tell what you liked about the other suggestions.

- While reading a book chapter, have students pick one of the characters (or an assigned character), and write a journal about what happens in each chapter from that character's point of view.

- Prepare statements for students to read about a character, event, or situation from any reading (story, book, poem, article, science book), for example, "Of all the events in this chapter, Toby finding the sack of gold was the most important." Now students have to agree or disagree and give supporting details. Then read others' arguments and respond to their ideas in comments.

- Have students write "Pass It On" stories. Each student begins a story based on individual choice of topic or theme or book the teacher assigns. The student writes for a certain length of time or number of words and then saves and posts the incomplete story. Students are then assigned another student's story to continue (if students sit in groups, it can be the person to the right or left, for example, and then just continue around the group). The next student cuts and pastes the incomplete story and writes the next part. You continue this process of "passing on" the story until it comes back to the original author (after two to five others have worked on it), who then writes the ending to the story, edits it, and posts the now completed story. The story appears on the original author's blog with the name of everyone who worked on the story and an explanation of the process.

- Try the same "Pass It On" story idea with a class or classes anywhere in the world. Come up with a way to keep track of who is going to work on which story along the way.

Mathematics

Although math might not immediately make us think of blogging, many math teachers have used blogging quite successfully as a way to have students explain their ideas.

- Post a problem and have students blog the results and explanation. Videos and diagrams can be uploaded as a blog.

- Have students create word problems using the skill you are working on. Comments can be the solution to the problem.

- Have students take turns summarizing the learning for the day. This gives the writer a chance to analyze and synthesize ideas, while giving the readers an opportunity to review the day's work.

- Have students write about what they are having difficulty understanding, and ask for clear explanations that will help them. Assign this for home-work one night; and the next night, assign commenting so explanations can be written.

- Have students who already demonstrate ability to understand a certain type problem or concept write the explanation and steps to solving the problem or understanding the concept so that any student could follow— or so a student one or two grades below theirs might be able to get it because other students have made it so simple to understand. This then becomes a resource for students at school or home.

Social Studies

Social Studies is a great subject to allow students to offer opinions of past and current world events.

- Post a political speech, article, or cartoon and respond to it.

- Write a diary entry about the historical events you are studying.

- Write comparisons between your own culture and a culture you are studying. Then find and invite teachers from those countries to have their students comment on your blogs.

- Draw a picture of a historical event or location, and post it along with a written explanation of how your picture depicts the event or location accurately.

- Research and post about the original inhabitants of the area where you live. Find out how they built their homes and how they survived the elements. Tell about the climate, what foods they ate and how they obtained food, tools, culture, when the area was settled, and so on. Encourage other bloggers to do the same. Then, using the information posted on other schools' blogs, compare and contrast the two locales. Make and post a Venn diagram that records the similarities and differences. You can share with as many schools as you have time for.

- Have you done "State" or "Country" reports? Think of doing blog reports about your state or country and then using them to teach others while they teach you about their state or country from their blogs. You can include links to informational websites about the history, people, famous or popular sites, photos, video, and so on. Then visit other participants' blogs to learn, comment on, and ask questions about the learning they've provided. A switch-up on this would be to do research on another class's state or country while they do yours, and then report to each other what you learned.

- Use your blog to ask questions about others' locations to gather information.

- Contact an expert or experts on any social studies topic you are studying, and ask them to respond to questions students research and post on their blogs.

- Have students write posts telling political candidates about the issues that are important to them. These are not posts supporting a certain candidate, but statements about what students feel are the biggest issues that require attention from whoever wins. You might contact the candidates' election committees and make them aware of the students' posts—they just might get some feedback.

Science

Science is perfect for blogs, allowing students to write about their hypotheses, experiments, and research.

- Write a plan for an experiment to be performed the next day.

- Outline the steps to an experiment, and ask others to perform the same experiment in their various locations and report back their results or findings. For example, it could be measuring the length of a shadow at a certain time of day to see if there are differences in other latitudes and longitudes around the world. Or have students from around the world grow and measure plants. Then analyze the results to draw conclusions about the data (for example, determine that one school location is a desert based on the lack of precipitation). Students post their conclusions. Photographs could be shared to accompany the measurements to chart growth or other findings.

- Write about the results of an individual or group experiment.

- Watch a video of an experiment and write about the results.

- Write a summary of the day's lesson.

- Post about your experiences, observations, and learning from a science activity, such as dissecting a flower or owl pellet, or a presentation to the class about snakes (or any other topic) by a guest speaker.

- Search for and find the best websites on the topics you are studying (for example, animal adaptations or Mars or atoms), based on the information they contain (related to the standards that you've shared with the class). Analyze and rate the websites for (1) completeness of information, (2) readability by a student of your students' age, and (3) any support photos, videos, audio files, or games the site may contain. Then post the top three to five links on a blog post in descending order from the best first, and explain why you chose them. This could be a group project as well. Students can then investigate the sites others have found.

- Find games online that teach about a science topic or concept being studied and write reviews, linking to the games.

Health

Health blogs can be a great venue for collecting information about life skills.

- Summarize the day's learning.

- Review health websites.

- Write goals for the year, and keep track of how you achieve those goals.

- Write public service announcements about drugs, smoking, dangerous dieting, and so on.

- Find a game online that teaches about a health topic or concept being studied, and write a review about it and link to it. Tell whether it is fun, is challenging, and teaches about the topic well.

- Post about your reaction and learning from a lesson or guest speaker's presentation on smoking or other health issues.

- Have students turn their blogs into information portals on public health subjects and issues. Provide links to web pages, photos, videos, and other information to make it easy for readers to find out about being healthy (smoking, drugs, exercise).

Physical Education

Blogging gives physical education teachers a way to assess students' knowledge about skills and concepts learned in class.

- List exercises you will follow, and keep a record in the comments about how often you follow the regimen.

- Watch a sports game, and write about the plays used, scores earned, and so on.

- Write about the history of a sport you are studying.

Art

Blogging is a super way to have students discuss art and artists.

- Post pictures from an artist, and have students opine about them.

- Embed a VoiceThread of different pictures, and have students voice their interpretations.

- Write biographies of artists.

- Post original artwork, and ask your audience for feedback.

- Find websites about a certain artist, type, or style of art or art history, and make a blog post that includes the links.

- Connect with another class, and share artwork on the same or different art activity or piece.

Music

Audio files lend themselves well to blogs.

- Post audio files of songs, and have students write the names of instruments they hear and notes and tempos they can identify.

- Write biographies of artists.

- Post original music in the style of an artist you are studying.

- Post your favorite song and explain why you like this music.

- Post about the meaning of the lyrics to a song.

- Post about what mood, setting, or meaning a piece of music represents or portrays.

- Have students find a song or musical piece that they feel best portrays a time or setting or any aspect you choose. Have them write responses about their choices.

- Share an audio file of your class singing or performing your school, state, or country 's anthem.

Character Education

Many of us today teach character education as part of our day. Use blogging as a way for students to think about character traits.

- Have students reflect on books or videos you watch in class.

- Have students reflect on videos you post.

- Explain how you exhibit a specific trait. Ask your audience to think about how they follow this trait.

- Write about the trait you find most important. Explain why it is so important.

- Write about the trait you find most difficult to exhibit. Explain why.

- Have students find a video or story online that teaches about a character trait, blog the link, and explain why others should watch it.

Foreign Language

Use your blog to practice language skills. Of course, all blogs should be written in the language being taught. Students might also record themselves speaking the language and post the audio files for comment.

- Post a simple quiz. Have students blog the answers.

- Post a list of words and have students use those words to write a story.

- Write a summary of the day's events.

- Have students write and post the same piece in English and in the language they are learning after they have translated it accurately.

- Have students translate posts written by classmates or students from another school into the language they are studying.

- Have students identify well-known poems, song lyrics, or sayings that are written in the language they are studying.

Connect with Other Bloggers

These are just some examples of content area blog assignments to get you started. Finding other bloggers and seeing what assignments they give out is another great way to get ideas. Connecting with bloggers in your content area also creates a ready-made audience for your students. It is vital to connect with others when blogging in order to maximize the value of conversing with others outside of the classroom. By your third blog, you should have an audience beyond your four walls. In the next chapter, we'll explore ways of finding other bloggers.

8

Commenting
and
Connecting

*Conversation is the laboratory and
workshop of the student.*

—Ralph Waldo Emerson

Writing a blog post and then seeing it
published for the world to read is an exciting
event and a dream motivator for your
students. If you have witnessed student
reactions when they are published, you know
what an excellent motivational tool blogging
can be to inspire student writers. And at first,
you might be satisfied with this one motivational aspect.

Then you remember that blogs are not just one dimensional. There's that commenting thing! More chances to read and write (and students are excited about it—what could be better?). Others read your students' posts and leave comments that students then read and write a response to. And, students read other blogs and leave comments for other blog authors. Watch what happens in your classroom when the first outside comments are received by your students. Once they've been bitten by the "comment bug," there's no going back. Some days you can just assign the class to read others' blogs and leave comments, and then smile when they respond enthusiastically.

Developing Communication Skills

Beyond all the excitement elicited, commenting on blogs is an important skill. It moves blogs from a simple writing assignment to a conversation. Comments allow readers to add their own ideas to the writing, make suggestions, and connect with the blogger. Your job as an educator is to help students make these connections, adding intelligent comments that elevate the conversation to a higher level, while monitoring their work. *Commenting is probably the most difficult part of student blogging.* Students quickly catch on to blogging, enjoying the audience, improving their writing skills, and learning to complete assignments thoughtfully. But comments are harder to understand. For students to comment appropriately, they have to make a connection to another blog and the blogger. It isn't always easy for students to accomplish this task.

The best way to begin is to start with comments within the classroom. One teacher we know spends time each day having students share small moments in their lives via a share post. Then three or four students will comment on the post. Sammy may share about the time she went to an amusement park and rode a rollercoaster for the first time. The comments might come out like these:

> **Student 1:**
> I really felt like I was there with you when
> you described the rollercoaster.

- This is an ideal comment. The student gave an example of a part of the share he connected to and told Sammy what she did well in her story-telling. She now knows what to continue doing in her shares.

> **Student 2:**
> Your share reminded me of the time I went on
> my first rollercoaster.
>

- This comment could lead to another share. If this were in writing (comments can be oral or written), student 2 now has a blog to write.

> **Student 3:**
> That was awesome.
>

- This comment is limited. In our classes, a comment such as this is called a "penny comment." It is short and has little value. This comment does not push the sharer to improve, does not tell the sharer what she did well, and makes no connections that allow for further shares. The class looks instead for "dollar comments."

> **Student 4:**
> I was really confused when you were talking
> about the amusement park. I didn't understand
> where you were. You didn't explain it well.
>

- While this comment gives Sammy some valuable information about how to share, it is unwarranted advice and does not belong as a comment unless the post author specifically requested this kind of input. The students learn through this activity that unless criticism is requested, none is given during a share.

As you can see, through this activity, students learn how to comment respectfully and helpfully. They also learn how to continue a conversation.

10
Student Blogging Guidelines

Kim Cofino, a 21st-century literacy specialist in the International School Bangkok in Thailand, had her fourth grade students create blogging and commenting guidelines for the students. These 10 guidelines are valuable for all bloggers.

You can find them at http://mscofino. edublogs.org/2009/09/06/student-blogging-guidelines/.

Another teacher models comments by commenting himself on the first student blog posts. By asking questions to further their understanding, making connections to the blog, and suggesting other blogs they might want to look at, he is modeling for the students how to comment themselves.

You can also use other class time to teach comments. During reading, comment about a book you are sharing. "I like this book because the author makes me feel like I am with her at school." Comment about writing the students are working on. "I enjoyed reading the section where you wrote about your dad. It made me laugh out loud." Comment about behavior in the classroom. "I am impressed with how many of you got your supplies ready without being reminded." The goal is to teach students to expand their ideas beyond "I like your blog." Model that elaboration in your language.

Reinforce the idea of respect and online etiquette (netiquette). Students often forget that there is a real person who has feelings at the other end of the computer. Students also often think they are anonymous when online and can therefore post anything they wish. They need to recognize the fact that someone worked hard on the blog and deserves consideration. Common early comments often deal with how the blog should be improved. "You spelled many words wrong," "You need to make this blog more interesting," and "This blog is boring" are often comments fielded in the first few weeks. Be sure to have students understand that, by the time the blog is posted, it has been edited to the best of the writer's ability. It is not up to them to critique it unless the blogger has specifically asked for criticism. And even then, criticism should be constructive.

Use this time to reinforce the idea of dollar comments versus penny comments. Early comments tend to be simple and do not move the conversation forward at all. "Awesome," "Neat blog," and "Cool" are examples of this. Being specific allows the writer to understand why the reader found the blog "awesome," "neat," or "cool." Instead of just one word, a comment can be, "I find it awesome that you have visited the Grand Canyon and learned so much about erosion. When I went to the Grand Canyon, I wasn't thinking about erosion at all." Now the blogger can continue the conversation. Maybe the blogger will post pictures as comments to that blog. Maybe the blogger will ask the commenter what he or she learned on his/her last vacation. Maybe another commenter will come along and mention erosion on mountaintops. We now have two or three bloggers discussing learning during a vacation, all because the first commenter didn't stop at "awesome."

Often we find that students are motivated to write a post in response to another post they read. Perhaps a student writes a post about the presidential election. He gives his opinion of a candidate, expressing concern about his ability to lead the country. Another student reads this blog and decides that she has more to say than just a simple comment. She decides to blog about why this candidate would make a good president. This conversation could end there. But good bloggers understand how to link the blogs. So Blogger B writes her post, beginning with a sentence explaining that her post is in response to Blogger A. She hyperlinks to Blogger A's blog. She then goes back to Blogger A and leaves a comment with a link to her blog, explaining that she has written a response in her own blog. Blogger A then goes to Blogger B's blog to see the response. In the meantime, any other students reading either blog can follow this conversation and contribute to it through commenting or through their own blogs. A simple writing assignment about the presidential candidate has turned into quite a high-level conversation.

Of course, all parties involved in this conversation have learned with their teachers how to be respectful and considerate. So, even though the students disagree, there is no name calling, nastiness, or bullying going on.

How to Find Other Bloggers

Grandmother used to say, "You have to write 'em to get 'em," when, as kids, we would complain about not getting many letters. How do you find other bloggers to start conversations with, ensuring that your students will receive comments on a regular basis? The key is to find other established blogs that match the subject or grade level you are looking for.

There are lists of school blogs online you can search through to find a match for your students:

SupportBlogging.com
http://supportblogging.com/Links+to+School+Bloggers

> This wiki, started by Steve Hargadon of Lincoln, California, has listings of educational blogs, both for the classroom and for teachers. Be sure to click on Classroom Blogs to find a listing of blogs you can send your students to.

Educational Blogs You Should Be Investigating
http://mrssmoke.onsugar.com/2787268

> This blog, written by Dyane Smokorowski, (aka MrsSmoke) from Andover, Kansas, has listings of educational blogs set up by subject and grade level.

Education Blogs by Discipline
http://movingforward.wikispaces.com/Education+Blogs+by+Discipline

> Scott McLeod, college professor and former administrator from Ames, Iowa, started this wiki. The blogs here are set up by discipline.

When you find a good match, search that blog's front page for links to additional blogs (this is called a "blogroll"). These are other blogs that the blog author has found and enjoyed. These blogs just might be a good match for you, too. And guess what? As you check out some of those blogs, they will also post blogrolls, and some of those will be different, and, well, you see where this goes. As you are perusing, also note any posts that might be on similar subjects or events that your students could blog about. Now you have those connections for your students you were searching for! Have them read the posts on these new blogs and leave comments. The more comments on blogs they leave, the more connections they make, and the more possible comments they will get in return. ("You have to write 'em to get 'em.")

If you are connected to other teachers through social networking sites such as Twitter, Facebook, or wikis, you have a great place to find other classrooms that blog. Just put out the word that you are looking for students to blog with on your subject or grade level or even a specific topic or book your class is reading. If you are not already networking online with other teachers and educators, you are missing out on a powerful resource. You can find resources and answers to questions on every aspect of teaching and learning and make connections with teachers and classrooms worldwide. Others with varying degrees of experience can help you and relate to what you are doing. We find making and nurturing these online connections the most consistently dynamic and valuable professional development and networking resources we have experienced. These sorts of connections are often called a professional learning network (PLN) or community of learning.

Also watch for blogging projects or topics that pop up from time to time. You will usually find out about them from posts on those other blogs you are following, and if you are networking online with other educators, they will spread the word, too.

Seven Random Facts—Dragonbloggers

http://classblogmeister.com/blog.php?blog_id=
968871&mode=comment&blogger_id=100229

Seven Random Facts is an example of a great blog project.

Student Blogging Challenge

http://wyatt67.edublogs.org/student-blogging-challenge

The Student Blogging Challenge is another great project to connect your students to others.

Bringing Us Together

http://studentfriends.edublogs.org

A great place to find out about challenges and projects is from the Bringing Us Together blog.

This is great! Your students are blogging, reading and commenting on other blogs, and getting comments back. Well, it can be even better!

9

Assessment

Everything that can be counted does not necessarily count; everything that counts cannot necessarily be counted.

—Albert Einstein

Assessment. Is there a word that causes more angst in education today?

"How do I get grades from this?" is on every teacher's mind. If you are used to grading student writing, projects, and presentations, you will probably have few issues with assessing blogs. The reality is that you assess blog posts the same way you would assess any other piece of work. Just be sure your students know the expectations beforehand. We often post a checklist of expectations (similar to the ones below) right into our blog assignments. This allows students to have a ready reminder of what they will be graded on.

Why is Reading Important?

A teacher we know, Mrs. Hensley, recently wrote a post on her blog about why she thinks reading is important. This is a great question to ask ourselves from time to time. Beyond the obvious, that reading well gets us good grades in school and makes our parents happy, why is reading important? What do we get from reading that we can't get from movies or pictures or other art forms? Since we are learning about personal essays in writing, let's make this blog a personal essay. So think of a big idea that answers the question "Why is reading important?" Then give personal examples to prove your big idea. If you look at Mrs. Hensley's blog, you will see how she did this very thing. She came up with an answer to the question and then examples from her life to explain the answer. While writing this blog, keep the following in mind:

1. Your introductory paragraph should name your big idea, which answers the question. It should also include at least three examples explaining your big idea. Each paragraph following should be about one example.

2. Each example paragraph should contain a small moment, told bit by bit.

3. You should have a concluding paragraph that ends your blog in an interesting way.

4. Use voice and vocabulary to make your blog interesting to your readers.

5. Stay focused and organized.

6. Edit carefully for spelling, punctuation, capitalization, and grammar.

7. Add pictures and/or video to enhance your piece.

This blog assignment is due on Monday, April 12th. If you wish to get suggestions for improvement, the blog must be submitted by Thursday, April 8th. Your graphic organizer for this blog is due on Wednesday, April 7th. The graphic organizer will be part of your grade.

Writing Quality or Content Knowledge?

If the blog post is primarily a writing assignment, it can be assessed for a grade as you would any writing assignment. Usage, punctuation, spelling, traits, and content are all important points to look at. As each new skill is taught, it is added to the expectations. For example, at the beginning of the year, the primary goals are editing skills and staying focused on a topic. So that is all the students are graded on. As organization, voice, vocabulary use, and other writing skills are taught, those skills are added to the checklist and (therefore) graded.

If, however, the writing was done in a content area such as math, science, or social studies, then you have other options. These blogs should be graded based on the content knowledge demonstrated. Giving your students a rubric or checklist with clear expectations is still a good idea. The rubric could state what grade will be given dependent on the facts included, the quality of explanations, charts, illustrations, and so on. You can still assess the piece as a writing assignment as long as students are aware of that beforehand. Just keep in mind that the blog is being used as a way to demonstrate knowledge. It is not different from a project handed in or a paper presented at the end of class. So the scoring shouldn't be any different.

If the writing piece is also to be presented orally, then grades can be assigned on quality of presentation. These can include projecting voice, clear speech, pacing, expression, eye contact, and sharing pictures, graphs, charts, and so on. Just keep in mind that you should take the time to teach and provide practice on these important skills before assessing them. A great way to involve the class is to have them take notes about the strengths and weaknesses on display and share them with the presenter. Again, spend time teaching and discussing that being supportive of each other is important and how presenting to a group is difficult and scary to most. This is another important learning piece that is often given short shrift in today's classrooms. It is a bit time consuming. However, students really do improve and gain confidence from these experiences in a safe, supportive environment. Technology has made it much more probable that we will all be up in front of others sharing information or content, even more so for our students, so it is important that we provide the experience and training in doing it well. If your students share with others using audio- or videoconferencing, you can use these same assessments.

Portfolios of student work are invaluable. Blogs are a great way to have an online portfolio. If you use blogs for writing skills, you, your students, and your students' parents will easily be able to compare earlier work to current work to see progress in different writing areas. If you are using your blog for content area work, you will have a timeline of work demonstrating knowledge. Imagine a science blog where students are asked to write up the results for each lab they complete in school. Your blog will allow you to see progress in use of science terminology, correlations to the real world, and clarity of ideas. By the end of the year, you will easily be able to see how much your students have learned without having to keep copies of labs and pulling out a fat folder of work for each grading period.

Portfolio of Progress

Imagine a geometry class. It is October, and the students are asked to write a proof. You post the assignment online, and the students respond with their answers as comments. Maggie completes the assignment, and her statements and reasons are correct. However, she labeled parts of her diagram incorrectly, and you are not really sure if she fully understood the problem. John completes half the assignment and stops. He is unable to make the connection between prior knowledge and new concepts. Anne completes the proof but makes some vital errors while doing so. It is clear that she has not learned the definitions of important terms such as congruency and similarity. You score the proofs accordingly and reteach as needed.

Now it is December. You have assigned many proofs, and it is time to post the last one before report cards are written. You wait for the responses. Maggie remembers to label her work properly. John finishes the whole assignment. He makes some errors, but he is recalling theorems correctly. Anne has now learned the definitions of terms and is able to write the proof correctly.

It is report card time. Parents are coming in for conferences, and you need to support your grades. All you have to do is open the blogs. They clearly show that Maggie deserves her A, John has moved into the C range, and Anne has finally earned her B. The blog was a helpful portfolio of the students' growth in writing and understanding proofs.

~~~

So blogs themselves become a portfolio or archive of student work. In writing, however, blog posts are often finished pieces, resulting from multiple drafts. We recommend you keep files of draft copies of individual student writing. You, your students, and their parents will appreciate being able to see the growth being made. One telling aspect is how many drafts were required initially to get a piece of writing to publishable status and how many fewer drafts are required as the student gains experience. Give students time occasionally to examine their files. This is often a very animated class period as students note the mistakes, vocabulary, usage, and voice they used initially. Have students make presentations in parent conferences by sharing pieces in chronological order. Students can make the case for their improvement by selecting representative pieces to showcase their progress. This can also be a method for students to construct goals for future improvement. In content areas, these portfolios can be used to note or chart students' understanding of concepts and learning during a unit of study and aid in assigning a grade.

Self-evaluation is a very powerful assessment tool, especially if you archive student self-assessments. You or students can maintain a file of dated self-evaluations. These should be reviewed from time to time so growth can be noted. Students can file rubrics, goals for improvement, lists of everyday words they misspell that they will be held accountable for, and more. If you use rubrics, they can be used as self-evaluation pieces. Have students use the rubric themselves or during a short conference with you. This is a great way for students to see how they could improve their work before it is actually due.

Just remember, blogging is not an add-on. Whatever achievements were required before are still required. You just have a different tool for gathering data. Grade your blogs the same way you would have graded the worksheets, lab assignments, and/or reports. Give out checklists beforehand so students know what is expected, and keep track of improvement along the way.

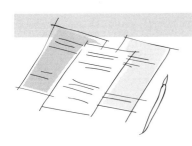

APPENDIX A

Sample Consent Forms

Disclaimer: The following forms are samples only and no guarantee is made or implied as to their legality in your school or district.

Form A-1: Technology Agreement (Sample AUP)

The Sample School District Elementary School
Student/Parent Technology Agreement

Please read this document carefully and review it with your student before signing.

The District's Acceptable Use Policy (AUP) prevents unauthorized access and other unlawful activities by users online, prevents unauthorized disclosure of or access to sensitive information, and complies with the Children's Internet Protection Act (CIPA). The District will use technology protection measures to block or filter, to a practical extent, access to any material that the District, in its sole discretion, believes to be unlawful, obscene, pornographic, and/or harmful to minors over the network. The District reserves the right to monitor users' online activities and to access, review, copy, and store or delete any electronic communication or files and disclose them to others as it deems necessary. Educators may use the Internet during class-directed group demonstrations with or without parental consent. Users should have no expectation of privacy regarding their use of District property, network and/or Internet access or files, including email.

Terms and Conditions of Use

1. **Privileges.** The use of the computer is a privilege, not a right, and inappropriate use may result in cancellation of those privileges.

   - Inappropriate sites will initially be identified by Information Technology

   - Access to technology may be revoked for inappropriate use.

   - Criminal actions may be pursued for illegal use of technology.

2. **Responsibilities.** Technology (including the use of the Internet) can be an exciting adventure for students. However, they must be responsible to:

   - Report to an appropriate adult (parent, teacher, or administrator) any inappropriate use of the Internet or any destruction of District property.

   - Any monetary costs incurred from misuse of equipment.

3. **Network Etiquette.** Students are expected to abide by the generally accepted rules of network etiquette. These include (but are not limited to) the following:

   - Never send, or encourage others to send, threatening or abusive messages.

   - Do not bully or harass another person.

   - You may be alone with your computer, but what you say and do can be viewed globally! Never swear, use profanity, vulgarities, or any other inappropriate language.

(Continued)

Form A-1 *(Continued)*

- Do not reveal any personal information, such as your full name, home address, or phone numbers, or those of others or your school site.

- Respect the rights of others. Do not do anything that degrades or disrupts the use of the network, either to the hardware, software, or others. Do not vandalize or destroy the data of another user. Do not use the school's network to gain unauthorized access.

- Do not attempt to bypass blocked Internet sites. If you feel a site that you should be allowed to view has been blocked, contact your teacher.

- Do not download, install, or run any programs unless specifically instructed by a teacher and then only under that teacher's supervision.

- Do not connect any devices to the computer without the consent of your teacher and then, only under the direct supervision of your teacher. This includes CDs, flash drives, iPods, PDAs, etc.

- All communications and information accessible via the network are subject to copyright law.

4. **Warranty**— The Sample School District makes no warranties of any kind, whether expressed or implied, for the service it is providing. The Sample School District will not be responsible for any damages you suffer. This includes loss of data resulting from delays, nondeliveries, misdeliveries, or service interruptions caused by its own negligence or your errors or omissions. Use of any information obtained via the Internet is at your own risk. The Sample School District specifically denies any responsibility for the accuracy or quality of information obtained through its services.

The signatures at the end of this document are legally binding and indicate that the signing party has read the terms and conditions carefully, understands their significance, and will abide by the Sample School District's Acceptable Use Policy. The parents' and student's signatures are required on this form.

☐ I allow my student to use the Internet at school.　　　　☐ I do not allow my student to use the Internet at school.

Student Name: _____

Student signature (if 18 or older): _____

Parent signature: _____

School: _____

Date: _____

Form A-2: Consent to Photograph Student

Sample School District
Media Services
Consent and Release Form

The Sample School District is seeking your approval to create and use **photographs and/or videotapes of you and/or your child** for educational purposes.

I (the undersigned), (please print) _____ ,

or parent/legal guardian of (please print) _____ ,

hereby authorize the Sample School District to photograph and/or videotape the person(s) listed above for educational purposes.

Student signature (if 18 or older) _____

Signature of parent/
legal guardian of student under 18 _____

Date: _____

Sample School District
123 Any Street Sample
Anytown, Anystate 00000

Form A-3: Consent to Post Student Work

Sample School District
Media Services
Consent and Release Form

The Sample School District is seeking your approval to have **your child's work (school-work, photo, video, writing, audio, and/or artwork)** posted on the Internet and the school's and school district's websites.

I (the undersigned), (please print) _____ ,

or parent/legal guardian of (please print)_____ ,

hereby authorize the Sample School District to post the child's work as described above for educational purposes.

Student signature (if 18 or older) _____

Signature of parent/
legal guardian of student under 18 _____

Date: _____

Sample School District
123 Any Street
Anytown, Anystate,

APPENDIX **B**

Respect and Acceptance Reading Resources

Picture Books—Stories

Crow Boy by Taro Yashima
 A boy is taunted by his classmates because he is different. By the end, his classmates learn to appreciate and respect him.

Elmer by David McKee
 A colorful elephant tries to be gray like the others but learns to accept himself the way he is.

Stand Tall, Molly Lou Melon by Patty Lovell
 A confident, tiny, clumsy girl moves to a new school and must learn to prove to herself and her classmates that she is worthy of respect.

Odd Velvet by Mary Whitcomb
 An odd girl teaches her classmates to appreciate their own uniqueness.

One Green Apple by Eve Bunting and Ted Lewin
 A Muslim girl, new to America, goes on a field trip with her class to an apple farm, where all the children learn to respect differences.

The New Kid by Katie Couric
 A new student in school is excluded by classmates until one girl finds out he is pretty much just like everyone else.

Fiction Chapter Books

Sahara Special by Esme Raji Codell
 A talented girl who receives special education services in school learns to accept herself.

Stargirl by Jerry Spinelli
 The new tenth grader arrives to school from a home school experience. The high schoolers bent on conformity learn about differences.

Maniac Magee by Jerry Spinelli
A homeless kid with above-average thinking and athletic skills works to bring a town split by race and ignorance together.

The Girl with 500 Middle Names by Margaret Peterson Haddix
A poor girl moves to a rich neighborhood and creates a story about herself to fit in.

The Gold Threaded Dress by Carolyn Marsden
A fourth grade girl moves to America from Thailand and struggles to fit in.

Nonfiction Chapter Books

People by Peter Spier
This book has beautiful illustrations that clearly demonstrate the differences among us.

Children Around the World by Donata Montanari
This brightly illustrated book focuses on the differences and similarities in children around the world.

Faith by The Global Fund for Children
This book of photographs shows ways in which the world celebrates and practices religious beliefs, focusing on the common threads.

If the World Were a Village by David J. Smith
This book breaks down the world into a village of 100 people, exploring the percentages for people with electricity, enough food, etc.

APPENDIX

C

National Educational Technology Standards

NETS for Students (NETS•S)

All K–12 students should be prepared to meet the following standards and performance indicators.

1. Creativity and Innovation

Students demonstrate creative thinking, construct knowledge, and develop innovative products and processes using technology. Students:

  a. apply existing knowledge to generate new ideas, products, or processes

  b. create original works as a means of personal or group expression

  c. use models and simulations to explore complex systems and issues

  d. identify trends and forecast possibilities

2. Communication and Collaboration

Students use digital media and environments to communicate and work collaboratively, including at a distance, to support individual learning and contribute to the learning of others. Students:

  a. interact, collaborate, and publish with peers, experts, or others employing a variety of digital environments and media

  b. communicate information and ideas effectively to multiple audiences using a variety of media and formats

  c. develop cultural understanding and global awareness by engaging with learners of other cultures

  d. contribute to project teams to produce original works or solve problems

3. Research and Information Fluency

Students apply digital tools to gather, evaluate, and use information. Students:

  a. plan strategies to guide inquiry

  b. locate, organize, analyze, evaluate, synthesize, and ethically use information from a variety of sources and media

c. evaluate and select information sources and digital tools based on the appropriateness to specific tasks

d. process data and report results

4. Critical Thinking, Problem Solving, and Decision Making

Students use critical-thinking skills to plan and conduct research, manage projects, solve problems, and make informed decisions using appropriate digital tools and resources. Students:

a. identify and define authentic problems and significant questions for investigation

b. plan and manage activities to develop a solution or complete a project

c. collect and analyze data to identify solutions and make informed decisions

d. use multiple processes and diverse perspectives to explore alternative solutions

5. Digital Citizenship

Students understand human, cultural, and societal issues related to technology and practice legal and ethical behavior. Students:

a. advocate and practice the safe, legal, and responsible use of information and technology

b. exhibit a positive attitude toward using technology that supports collaboration, learning, and productivity

c. demonstrate personal responsibility for lifelong learning

d. exhibit leadership for digital citizenship

6. Technology Operations and Concepts

Students demonstrate a sound understanding of technology concepts, systems, and operations. Students:

    a. understand and use technology systems

    b. select and use applications effectively and productively

    c. troubleshoot systems and applications

    d. transfer current knowledge to the learning of new technologies

NETS for Teachers (NETS•T)

All classroom teachers should be prepared to meet the following standards and performance indicators.

1. Facilitate and Inspire Student Learning and Creativity

Teachers use their knowledge of subject matter, teaching and learning, and technology to facilitate experiences that advance student learning, creativity, and innovation in both face-to-face and virtual environments. Teachers:

    a. promote, support, and model creative and innovative thinking and inventiveness

    b. engage students in exploring real-world issues and solving authentic problems using digital tools and resources

    c. promote student reflection using collaborative tools to reveal and clarify students' conceptual understanding and thinking, planning, and creative processes

    d. model collaborative knowledge construction by engaging in learning with students, colleagues, and others in face-to-face and virtual environments

2. Design and Develop Digital-Age Learning Experiences and Assessments

Teachers design, develop, and evaluate authentic learning experiences and assessments incorporating contemporary tools and resources to maximize content learning in context and to develop the knowledge, skills, and attitudes identified in the NETS•S. Teachers:

   a. design or adapt relevant learning experiences that incorporate digital tools and resources to promote student learning and creativity

   b. develop technology-enriched learning environments that enable all students to pursue their individual curiosities and become active participants in setting their own educational goals, managing their own learning, and assessing their own progress

   c. customize and personalize learning activities to address students' diverse learning styles, working strategies, and abilities using digital tools and resources

   d. provide students with multiple and varied formative and summative assessments aligned with content and technology standards and use resulting data to inform learning and teaching

3. Model Digital-Age Work and Learning

Teachers exhibit knowledge, skills, and work processes representative of an innovative professional in a global and digital society. Teachers:

   a. demonstrate fluency in technology systems and the transfer of current knowledge to new technologies and situations

   b. collaborate with students, peers, parents, and community members using digital tools and resources to support student success and innovation

   c. communicate relevant information and ideas effectively to students, parents, and peers using a variety of digital-age media and formats

   d. model and facilitate effective use of current and emerging digital tools to locate, analyze, evaluate, and use information resources to support research and learning

4. Promote and Model Digital Citizenship and Responsibility

Teachers understand local and global societal issues and responsibilities in an evolving digital culture and exhibit legal and ethical behavior in their professional practices. Teachers:

a. advocate, model, and teach safe, legal, and ethical use of digital information and technology, including respect for copyright, intellectual property, and the appropriate documentation of sources

b. address the diverse needs of all learners by using learner-centered strategies and providing equitable access to appropriate digital tools and resources

c. promote and model digital etiquette and responsible social interactions related to the use of technology and information

d. develop and model cultural understanding and global awareness by engaging with colleagues and students of other cultures using digital-age communication and collaboration tools

5. Engage in Professional Growth and Leadership

Teachers continuously improve their professional practice, model lifelong learning, and exhibit leadership in their school and professional community by promoting and demonstrating the effective use of digital tools and resources. Teachers:

a. participate in local and global learning communities to explore creative applications of technology to improve student learning

b. exhibit leadership by demonstrating a vision of technology infusion, participating in shared decision making and community building, and developing the leadership and technology skills of others

c. evaluate and reflect on current research and professional practice on a regular basis to make effective use of existing and emerging digital tools and resources in support of student learning

d. contribute to the effectiveness, vitality, and self-renewal of the teaching profession and of their school and community

INDEX

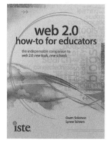